MW01047086

*One person's memory is another's forgotten.*
*Another's mistaken is another's remembered.*
*Piece by piece the past is present,*
*not to be confused with the future.*

—Timothy Williams

# Figure on the Road

## California Wildfires, Mountain Resorts,
## and a Lost Romantic Era

### Timothy Williams

JAXON'S
PRESS

"... we realize we are really just a bunch of small towns, joined by a common affection for people and the land."

– Carl Nolte, *San Francisco Chronicle*

Carl Nolte took note to remember the people who lost their lives in the wildfires (in an October 28, 2017, article). He wrote vignettes about each person: the young, the vibrant, and the elderly. He helped us all gather support for our collective tragedy by acknowledging, "They were all part of our family."[i]

# Figure on the Road

## California Wildfires, Mountain Resorts, and a Lost Romantic Era

Through the murk and chaos, I came upon
a figure on the road; closer scrutiny revealed that it was
the fountain on the embattled grounds of Starview Lodge.

# Acknowledgements

I would like to extend much gratitude to the following people who inspired and contributed to this book.

To the loving memories of my parents, Bob and Muriel Williams, and their lifelong friends, Roger and Bonnie Garety, Jim Gilmartin, Ed McGillicuddy, and Ivan Johnson.

Thank you, Beverly McGillicuddy, Casey Williams, Bailey Williams, John Flynn, Roddy Garety, and Rick and Carol Magill, for inspiration; and my brother, Jack Quintero, for his suggestion to expand on the Forest Lake Resort chapters.

Thank you, Sarah Estalee Baker, Michele Anna Jordan, E. Breck Parkman, Betty Rodgers, Cynthia Helen Beecher, Molly Brown, Chantel C. Lucier, Pierrette Montroy, Katy Dang, Nathan Elder, and Laurie Dawson for proofreading, use of language, and helping it all make sense.

Thank you, young firefighters, Genesis Soria and Owen Ogden Barlow, for your participation.

100 years of gratitude to Donna Hoberg for her historic contribution, her must-have book, *Resorts of Lake County*, by Arcadia Publishing.

Thank you to Barbara of Starview Lodge for her 2005 images and Wayne Darby (RIP) for his landscape painting.

**Editor-in-Chief Alison Jacobs Maldonado**
**Spanish translations by Alison Jacobs Maldonado**

**"All of the areas of historical existence are now on private lands.**
**Please respect the privacy of these properties and do not trespass."**
**– Richie Bucher, Firefighter**

Published by Jaxon's Press.  707 321-3852
timothytree@juno.com and jaxonspress@gmail.com
Copyright © 2021 Timothy Williams
All Rights Reserved.

♫

Second Edition
First Printing

Library of Congress Control Number: 2021923384
**ISBN 978-1-7378349-0-8**
**ISBN 978-1-7378349-1-5 (e-book)**
**ISBN 978-1-7378349-2-2 (audio book in progress)**

*For those who escaped the fires*
*to those who held their ground,*
*for the firefighters who have*
*looked out for so many.*

**The Palisades in Napa County (the southern part of the Mayacamas Mountain Range), on the way to Lake County.**

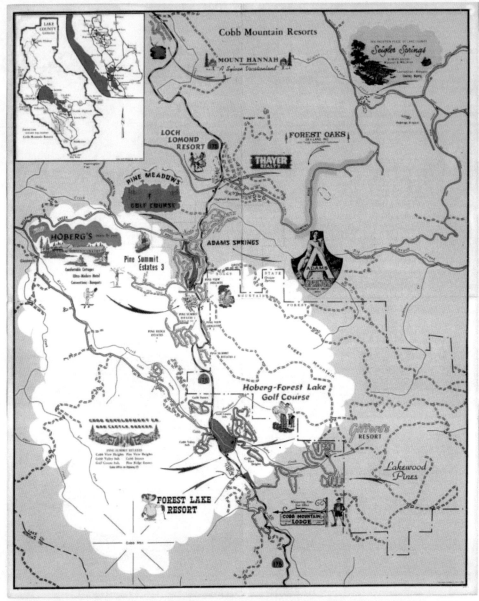

The above map, from a 1950s or '60s sales pamphlet for Cobb Development Company's Pine Summit Estates, reflects many of the resorts mentioned in this book. Lots were priced starting at $2,950, with a down payment of $100 and monthly payments of $29.50. Water use required a $20 share in Cobb Mutual Water Company and a flat rate charge of $2 per month. Property taxes were $35 to $45 per year. The company office was located on the corner of Golf Road and Highway 175 in the Middletown Fire District. Fire trucks were five minutes away.[ii]

# Contents

# Introduction

Lake County, its neighborhoods, communities, and landscapes have had a lasting impact on both my formative years and my entire adult life. Many of the stories in this book highlight my memories of summers on Cobb Mountain with my family in the 1950s and early '60s. The stunning scenery of Lake County has brought me back every year for decades, and nostalgia for my childhood summers has inspired me to jot down my most prominent memories: roadside cherry juice and fresh produce from local farms, jazz bands and packed dance halls, teens building self-esteem at the horse corral, juke boxes belting out chart-toppers across the lake, and Cobb's gold-standard treatment of its customers, to name a few.

As climate change began sweeping across California, making drought and wildfires the norm, my writing shifted towards poems about destroyed sacred trees, blackened hills, ravaged earth, and the longing for rainstorms to quench California's thirst. In turn, my journal entries began to document the horror of several wildfires—namely, the Valley,[1] Tubbs,[2] and Kincade[3] fires—the brownish clouds floating into our neighborhood, our emergency evacuation, the grit and bravery of the firefighters, and our somber return to Cobb Mountain to survey the devastation. As a testament to the tight-knit communities across Lake, Napa, and Sonoma counties, this book also covers the generous and compassionate response in the wildfires' aftermath, including music and artist benefits, all different kinds of donations, and websites for coordinating volunteers and events.

---

[1] September 12, 2015, in Lake County.
[2] October 8 through October 31, 2017, in Napa, Sonoma, and Lake Counties.
[3] October 23 to November 6, 2019, in Sonoma County.

In the wake of the wildfires, when memories from my life on Cobb Mountain came flooding back, I began thinking how my summers there shaped me. I don't remember much about the Widow Creek Fire of '62 that burned over 10,000 acres, but I learned to fire watch early in life. While my very first memories took place at Pine Grove Resort, most of the stories in the book occur around the cabin my parents, Bob and Muriel, built on High Road near Forest Lake—the resorts, trees, mountains, and lakes were a second home. I had the freedom to wake up at dawn and venture out to Forest Lake Resort. On one occasion, I took my 8-millimeter camera and followed a rangale of deer up the trail where the quail gathered and fed upon native blackberries. The expansive landscape was a creative haven for kids lucky enough to live on Cobb Mountain and spend an entire summer or just a week there. The 50-foot trees and breathtaking panoramas fueled many imaginations and allowed us the freedom to truly be children.

In my teen years during the early '60s, I began to learn the ways of the world. The county's resorts provided my friends and me with the opportunity to build a strong work ethic. Many of us sought employment at the resorts, where the breakfast shift started at six in the morning. We were expected to show up on time and do the job well enough to work another week—some kids lasted the whole summer and lived in dorms on the Forest Lake grounds. In my 20s, the resort lands offered something different, like discovering the zen of a golf round, strolling to the lakeside dock to reflect, or taking a long walk at dawn on Bottle Rock Road to observe random instances of natural occurrence. The terrain offered a fertile landscape for my imagination and the space to explore states of consciousness. It was the place where my love for the worlds of poetry and music joined forces.

In addition to reminiscing about my decades, the fires helped me appreciate the last few months of my father's life on Cobb Mountain, especially at Starview Lodge, where he dropped in to regale friends with stories, sip two drinks with fellow veterans, and head home alone. His wife—and my mother—Muriel Williams, had passed away in their South Hoberg home on Thanksgiving night in 1988; my father lay on one side and I sat on the other. While time spent at Pine Grove Resort marked the beginning of the Williams' family summers in Lake County, Starview Lodge symbolized the end. After my father became, in his words, "too old to live on Cobb anymore," he moved back to Santa Rosa to be closer to his family and doctors. Around that time, my wife, Sarah Baker, and I threw a party for Bob Williams' 80th birthday at Starview in 2004.

In the late summer of 2005, he returned to Cobb for the weekend. My son Casey Williams married Regina by the same last name. We rented the outdoor church space at Forest Lake Resort. Thanks to credentials from Universal Life Church, I read the invocation that Casey wrote and rang the church bell after their kiss. We held the reception at Loch Lomond on a pristine day. That was my dad's last overnight visit to Cobb until Casey and I carried his ashes from Sonoma County back to Starview. We sat with Van and Rick (the owner and his partner), and shared a soda Bob would have loved, mixed with vodka and a twist, in tall glasses. When Sarah and I returned to Cobb Mountain after the Valley Fire in 2015, I was thunderstruck when I saw the surviving statue in the fountain, radiant against the emptiness of the Starview grounds. The "figure on the road" then became the title of this book. Van and Rick, Starview and my dad. It was a swell period of time.

After Bob passed away, Sarah and I spent more time in Lake County. I recall the time we stayed four nights at the High Road cabin built in '62. As she worked on a jigsaw puzzle, she realized the beauty of Cobb and the power of nature. We walked across the road and found, overgrown and hidden by brambles, the slight waterfall where my family picked watercress. She threw her arms around me and said, "I don't want to go anywhere for a long time." We stood in our embrace as the water gushed down the hill from Schwartz Spring, ran under the road, tumbled over many moss-covered stones, wound down the Circle-of-Life Loop,[iii] raced past the firehouse, and poured into Cobb Village.

For a dozen years since then, we have spent half of every year in Cobb, reinventing ourselves while making a home of our own from a cabin built in 1962 by a man called Smitty. Besides working nonstop, it seems now, we have enjoyed the respite from city life in the quiet beauty of Lake County. When the 2020 pandemic hit, Cobb Mountain was our shelter from the storm. After investing many long hours creating our dream home, it raised the emotional and financial stakes even higher to think that all our time, attention, and investment could be burned to the ground in a matter of minutes. Several of the poems and stories in this book were inspired by our shared experiences in the fallout of the wildfires: sending romantic texts to each other when we were trapped in separate counties, enjoying a biking excursion a few hours before the Valley Fire, urgently packing to evacuate, returning to Cobb after a two-week evacuation, and facing the remains of cherished settings, homes, and resorts.

Finally, the survival and resiliency of a few Lake County resorts and locales were the impetus behind the last pieces of prose towards the end of this book: Pine Grove, Whispering Pines, Loch Lomond, Hardester's

Grocery, Cobb Pacific Gas Station, and others. These stories speak to the unity of not only the communities in Lake County but also to the collective relief efforts by volunteers, musicians, and artists in the neighboring counties of Napa and Sonoma. As sometimes divergent counties, the wildfires joined us as we persevered through the collective devastation.

Through my experience with reviewing years-old poetry and stories for inclusion in this book, I've found that revisiting the past is not only a search for something that has been lost, but is also a way to rediscover our ancestors' wisdom. (We have, after all, been part of Mother Earth for millennia.) While this book is not intended to be a Cobb history book, it is my hope that *Figure on the Road* serves as a reminder of Cobb Mountain's illustrious past, the abundant benefits of nature at all stages of its life, the deleterious effects of climate change, and the resorts' romantic era for its contribution to humanity and the spirit of joy.

**The Heart of Highway 29.**

# *Foreword*
## *by E. Breck Parkman*

I arrived in California in 1971, fell madly in love with the area, and stayed. To my formative eyes, California was truly the "Golden State." Within a few years, I took a position as a State Archaeologist with California State Parks. I was there for the next four decades. My work took me to all corners of the state and to many places around the world. It was the perfect job for me, in the perfect state. My research interests have always been broad and range from Ice Age megafauna to the archaeology of '60s hippie communes. I was able to do the eclectic style of archaeology I had always dreamed of. Along the way, I studied indigenous burning practices, participated in the state's prescribed fire plans, and wrote about the effects of global climate change during the Pleistocene/Holocene Transition. In addition to being a now-retired Senior State Archaeologist, I am a longtime Research Associate at the University of California at Berkeley and a Past President of the Society for California Archaeology. Currently, I sit on the Board of Directors of a local non-profit, the Sonoma Ecology Center.

I met Timothy Williams 30 years ago, when he became my accountant and, soon after, my friend. Over the years, Tim has also become both a mentor and an inspiration to me. I have attended his baseball games as well as his theatrical and musical performances. His performance of *Under Milk Wood* at the Main Street Theater (now Main Stage West) in Sebastopol still resonates with me, as does his performance of *A Child's Christmas in Wales*. I still enjoy listening to his album, *Lunch at Lola's*. And what is my favorite song on the album? "Cobb Mountain!"

The night of September 12, 2015, I sat spellbound at home, scanning social media for indications that Tim and his wife, Sarah Baker, had survived the Valley Fire. From an earlier post of his, I knew that he and Sarah were at their cabin on Cobb Mountain when the fire broke out. And I knew they had been forced to flee as flames moved perilously close. What I did not know was whether their evacuation had been successful. So, I sat and scanned Facebook for hours until I finally found what I was looking for—evidence that my friends had survived. Days later, I learned that their beloved cabin had survived as well. Unfortunately, not everyone was so lucky.

The Valley Fire burned 76,067 acres, forcing thousands of people to evacuate. The fire destroyed mountain communities and wildlands alike. Almost 2,000 structures were destroyed, including people's homes and places of business. Included were some of the resorts that had made Cobb Mountain famous. Four people lost their lives in the fire. Upon his return to Cobb Mountain, Tim took a long look at what the fire had done. He wanted to see for himself what the fire had taken and what it had left behind. In true poetic form, he made a record of his observations.

In *Figure on the Road*, Timothy brings his observations together to tell the story of Cobb Mountain, a place his family visited and then called home for several generations. Included are reminiscences of a childhood spent growing up on the mountain, a personal history of the resorts that are found there, and the terror of fleeing the Valley Fire. He reveals the fire's aftermath, with his striking impressions of the ravaged landscape.

At the time, the Valley Fire was one of the worst fires we had witnessed in the area. However, since 2015, California has seen even larger and more deadly blazes. In fact, the state's eight largest wildfires occurred in the years following the Valley Fire. That includes the currently active Dixie Fire, which to date has burned over 960,000 acres.

In 2017, the Nuns Fire burned within a mile of my home and forced me to evacuate. I was reminded of Tim and Sarah fleeing Cobb Mountain two years earlier. As I drove away, I feared I would not have a home to return to. I could see the fire consuming the hillside just above my neighborhood and home after home going up in flames. I was one of the lucky ones, though. I returned to an intact home, but I have dreaded the arrival of fire season ever since. Some Californians have had enough and are moving to less fire-prone states. This movement pales in comparison to some of the human migrations already occurring elsewhere in the world, as climate change begins to take its toll. Wildlife and plants are being forced to migrate. We are all in this together, all living things.

The fires are coming at a quickened pace now, and they burn hotter and seem to spread faster than before. They have become far more destructive, too. In recent years, the fire season has started earlier in the year and has lasted longer than in earlier times. What we are seeing is undoubtedly a result of climate change. There are various reasons for this change, but the effect of drought has played a major role in creating apocalyptic wildfires here in the American West. Continued drought has weakened the trees, making them more susceptible to bark-boring beetle infestations and other ailments. Dead and dying trees add fuel to wildfires. Record-breaking temperatures have marked our recent summers, resulting in hotter days and drier forests. It is a recipe for disaster. As summer approaches, we dread fire season, and we have grown to expect the worse.

In *Figure on the Road*, Timothy writes, "imagine a summer without fires." Those of us who are old enough can recall such summers. But while we can imagine a summer without fire, can we prevent catastrophic wildfires like we have seen in recent years? Climate change has brought about a new reality for California, and wildfires appear to be part of our new normal. Of the 20 largest wildfires in California's history, all but two occurred in the first two decades of the 21$^{st}$ century. The year 2020 was the most destructive wildfire season in California's history, with over 4 million acres burned. And to date, 2021 wildfires have burned more than 2.4 million acres. But that's small compared to what happened elsewhere in the world. From 2019 to 2020, close to 46 million acres burned in Australia, while in Siberia 64 million acres burned from March to the end of September 2020. Meanwhile, the Amazon lost nearly 5.6 million acres to fire that year.

Climate change and land-use changes are the primary causes of most of our recent catastrophic wildfires. Fire can be a good thing as it's an important part of the natural environment, but these are mostly unnatural conflagrations that we are seeing today. For example, take the recent fires in the Amazon. The fires have been set to clear the land to allow it to be used for ranching. The clearcutting of the Amazon for converting land to pasture for cattle has been going on since the 1960s. Ranching is the main cause of deforestation in Australia, too.

What can we do? For starters, we must think globally and act locally. Most of us have heard that saying before. More than ever, now is the time to embrace it. Embracing this mantra 50 years ago would have obviously been better but doing so now is imperative. We need to be aware of the coming crisis and how that will affect our neighborhoods and our world. As we work to adapt to climate change at home, we need to remain aware of what is happening elsewhere. It is our responsibility as citizens of Earth.

The population of our planet has tripled in my lifetime. And is increasing still. That kind of growth is not sustainable without a well-planned adaptation to climate change. For those of us living in California, in what is essentially "fire country," climate response must include a sense of fire culture. From a new understanding of fire comes better resiliency. We need to rethink how we live, where we build, and how we get from one place to another. We need to address California's insane housing market and we need to support a renewable energy transition. We need a more biodiverse and environmentally stable society and a bipartisan political coalition that appreciates what is driving climate change and has the intelligence and moral strength to con-front it. We need to decarbonize the sky and rewild the land.

*Figure on the Road* is well worth reading. You can read it easily in a single sitting or two. Timothy's poetry is touching, and his description of Cobb Mountain and the role the resorts played in the local history engages the reader, creating a sense of place that even those who have never visited Cobb Mountain will likely appreciate. This book will make you think about your own sense of place and those places most import-ant to you. Tim's writing takes a snapshot of a time and a place that are rapidly changing. His words, I believe, will make you think about climate change, and they will challenge you to make a difference.

Places like Cobb Mountain were important in the past. They were where we could go to appreciate clean air, still nights, and tall green trees. They were places worthy of our pilgrimage. They still are.

Sonoma, California<br>
December 19, 2021

The poster for the Merlot Theater variety event was designed by the generous artist and Poetry Band multi-instrumental lead guitarist, Kevin Haapala. Graphics by Al Ardelle. The painting of the sea goddess became the Poetry Band logo.

# The Spanish Translations in Figure on The Road

The Spanish language and the people who speak it are a large part of the history and culture of California and the United States, as well as our agriculture, cuisine, wine, and music. More specifically, the Mexican people have an indelible and valuable influence on our cultural landscapes, and in my part of California, bilingual signs are the norm. I have always included Spanish language translations of my poems and songs—not all of them, but rather the few that can be passionately illustrated for the reader and the listener.

Reading the Spanish-translated poems in *100 Love Sonnets* by Pablo Neruda has been a significant influence in my life. Neruda's love sonnets fit perfectly with music. And without any instrumentation, the sonnets contain their own musicality discovered in fathomed silences. His book has been my companion of study, wonder, and humility. It was written in the universal language of love with an almost, if not divine, respect for life itself. Since discovering *100 Love Sonnets,* music and poetry together have become my pathway to happiness and interconnection with others.

Another reason for being drawn to the Spanish language is that Mexican and Latino cultures have always been a part of my life. My mother's first husband was Native American and part Hispanic, and I was raised with their sons: my half-brothers, Steve (RIP) and Jack. Bob and Muriel were not Hispanic, but their love for Mexican food, people, and music was evident, so I grew up feeling connected and drawn to the culture. As a result of my taking two years of high school Spanish, I was able to find my way around Mexico in my late teens and 20s. As a young husband and father, my family and I settled into the culturally diverse South Park neighborhood in Santa Rosa. We lived down the street from a

Mexican family: an elderly woman, her daughter, and two granddaughters, Juanita and Josefina, who were constant companions to my son, Casey. I very much valued Casey's friendship with Johnny and Joey, as they were called, because I had grown up in San Rafael, where most of my neighborhood and friends were ethnically and culturally homogenous. The silver lining was that San Rafael was a short 17 miles from San Francisco, which was wholly diverse. The idea of breaking down barriers within our South Park community brought me joy and reminded me of the family ideals I carried back from The City,[4] as well as Mexico in the '60s.

Before a chilling divorce in 1990, I moved from my home in South Park and sadly said goodbye to Johnny and Joey's family. Though I did go back to visit, of course, it wasn't the same. A few years passed, and I greatly missed spending time in the old neighborhood, especially the walk to the Mexican restaurant around the corner, Mi Ultimo Refugio, which I frequented several times a year. Then—almost overnight—a referral from my friend Jim Gromo brought me back into close contact with the Mexican community of Santa Rosa. After driving my '68 Chevy truck, Ol' Jaxon, through a Highway 101 tunnel to Lola's Market in the Spanish-speaking part of town, I was once again surrounded by a community of warm, caring people who treated me, to a degree, like family. Lola herself would say, "You want a burrito, Timoteo? What kind do you want?" I felt like Lola's was a second home.

Around that time, I started thinking about a bilingual poetry and musical event. Through my connections in the community, I had the good fortune to record my song, "For the Red," with Mar y Paz of KBBF Radio and players from the Hispanic community. Later, Kevin Haapala, Mar y Paz, and I performed it live at Santa Rosa's Merlot Theater at

---

[4] Northern Californians often refer to San Francisco as "The City."

Luther Burbank Center for the Arts in 2002 before a mostly Hispanic audience. That one night made a lasting impression, and looking back on those days, I feel a huge gap—a loss, really—in my connection to the Mexican people.

For a time, I tried to connect once again with the Latinx community by looking for a Spanish translator for my poems. I bounced around between translators until I asked the right person, Chantel C. Lucier, a friend of Mexican descent from San Francisco, who recommended her college friend, Alison Jacobs Maldonado. I waited for years to find someone on the same page, like Alison, who translated these poems and worked as editor-in-chief of this book's final contents. Without the translated poems, this collection would be incomplete. These translations integrate conversations beyond everyday travels and take them into a world that has been and always will be a vibrant part of our cultural fabric.

**Windows of offices (left) and bar (right) look over the staircase and main entrance to Forest Lake Lodge.**

# It's a Hop, Skip, and a Jump to Forest Lake Resort

Long before the Vietnam War and the year 1968. Long before Cesar Chavez and Dolores Huerta founded the United Farm Workers Union and Robert Kennedy met with Chavez and announced his candidacy for president. Before Martin Luther King was shot in Memphis and Robert Kennedy in L.A., Forest Lake Resort held our innocent lives in the balance.

To get there, the classic American family of four or five drove from their homes—from the San Francisco Bay Area, Sacramento, and counties all over California—to take a gander at country life. And there was always someone from a small town nobody had ever heard of. Word got around about "The Switzerland of America,"[iv] the accessible alternative to Tahoe and its four or five hour drives.

In the generous Sonoma-Napa-Lake region of '62, produce from small farms was sold at fruit-and-vegetable stands. Driving west, outside Calistoga, past the Silverado Trail on Highway 29, a popular stand was filled with strawberries in the spring and Lake County pears in the fall. All the vegetables in season filled its bins. Glass bottles, paper bags, and wooden boxes abounded; plastic was not yet a ruthless epidemic of unending waste. Jugs of cherry juice made it an obligatory roadside stop. Today, one place that resembles these stands is just outside Sebastopol, California, at Andy's Produce, an open air grocery store with a vast array of fresh produce that offers fresh fish right from the docks of Bodega Bay. It continues to hold the magic of those bygone vegetable stands.

For wine sampling—as it was called back then—the places to go were the family-owned vineyards. Tasting wine didn't carry a fee. Very few of them thrive to this day. More have sold to corporations. For a price, you can still drop in any winery for a tour and taste the native Zinfandel. Then, however, boutique rooms and retail tastings didn't exist. On the long drives through farmlands, working windmills turned.

For the Williams family, the road to the Cobb Mountain resort lands began at the horseshoe turn on Highway 29 off Tubbs Lane.[v] At the time, Highway 29 was even more narrow than the two-lane road it is today. Further along was a flagpole that flew an American and a confederate battle flag. The latter disappeared in the '60s, thankfully becoming the last confederate flag seen flying on Highway 29. As resort-bound carloads got further along, near the Robert Louis Stevenson summit,[vi] taverns with opened doors cozied up to travelers.

Hot radiators sprang leaks on those steep mountain drives. Two resting spots, both sporting free outdoor water hoses, awaited in case a car drove up steaming. Inside, friendly folks worked behind the bar and served the small tables. Good spots to take a breather. They echoed with the sweet breeze of cold steel, lime drifted from a shaker of margaritas, and fiestas of popcorn aroma blended with grenadine syrup. A jukebox played the rich tremolo of guitar on the song, "Telstar," adding distance to the trip. After a spell by the blue windows and sunlit knotty-pine walls, we were back on the road and following the S turns, C curves, and the long-drawn-out question marks on the road to "The Switzerland of America." Along the drive, billboards read, "It's a Hop, Skip, and a Jump to Forest Lake Resort."

From there, we ascended Cobb Mountain, taking the steep Highway 175 climb from the classic western movie set of Middletown, past Anderson Springs and up to Shadow Brook, a hollow with gardens and cabins on three acres, where we stayed one winter night in the '60s for two dollars and fifty cents. Finally, we descended into Whispering Pines, past the infamous Four Nicks, a wild west bar complete with the occasional black eye,[vii] to where the road leveled out on a green corridor that paralleled an idyllic lake, and the temperature dropped slightly. The enveloping cool greeted the influx of curious travelers. Shade brought rewards of calm as did water and breeze, tell-tale signs that dispelled the exaggerated rumor of Lake County's relentless and unforgiving heat. Trees breathed; the breezes spoke to the warm arrivals of many faces, withered by the ride, yes, but congratulating each other for surviving the challenge.

In the '40s and early '50s, round-body cars, in shades of pollen yellow, lima bean green, crow black, and foggy-day gray, glided through. In the '60s, two-toned, extreme, and finned classics—with wide white-wall tires and ornate chrome hubcaps—rolled in. They dipped under the welcoming shaded entry of Forest Lake Drive and coasted beside the brook, past a pair of oak trees and a bench, and parked under the trees by the pool opposite the grand lodge. Near the pool was The Fountain (an old-fashioned soda fountain), an outdoor church, and a peewee golf course built by the artistic hands of Cobb's Jim McInnis, who included mosaics of native stone in his signature designs.

Around the diving board, the youth gathered. Girls, who seemingly possessed wings, performed arcs and back dives and entered the water quietly. Boys loudly competed and learned from older divers how to practice the art. A champion diver named Rick Deering was so gifted that even the cool teenagers tried to emulate him. He was of medium height, tanned, and had broad robust shoulders; his body and mind were designed for the pool. I haven't seen him for 20 years, but back then, he was a gymnastics coach at Sonoma State University.

3

Divers used to "cut" the board, that is, try to get as close to it as possible on the way down. One of the lifeguards, an excellent diver, good with the younger kids, too, and a hefty presence at the pool, took a jump and hit the board on the way down. He reached out his hand to shield his fall and to push away from the board. Because of the weight of his stout body, he couldn't pull it off, and his momentum carried him straight down; he scraped his chest and legs all the way to the pool! The few standing around watched in slow motion as the board peeled the hair from his body until he hit the water. We gathered around and jumped in, but he insisted he was all right. He climbed out of the pool, and by then, a few other people showed up to see. His hirsute body bore lacerated channels of raspberry skin, cutting roads all the way down his muscular physique.

Benches ran along poolsides, and the lawn ran along the pool and past it, joining a wide meadow with room for blankets and towels. On the right side was a tiled wading pool for the kiddies and pull-up jungle bars made out of pipes for the older kids. Across the road from the outdoor pool area stood the impressive lodge. As drivers drifted in, they slowed down to see patrons in shorts and swimming attire walking back and forth between the pool and the lodge. On some warm nights, they gathered 'round the phone—on a bench between two oak trees—and simply waited.

A man on one crutch, a war veteran missing an arm, appeared at the resort on occasion. He dressed immaculately in a pinstriped suit and sat quietly among the generations of folks listening to the music, watching people dancing and drinking on warm evenings when time lasted forever to the moon and stars. I am reminded of him each time I hear that line from Jimi Hendrix's song, "The Wind Cries Mary:" "And with this crutch, its old age and its wisdom." That veteran towered as a symbol of dignity for the gentlemen among us who were severely wounded—and even shell-shocked from the wars—and still joined the crowd.

**The oak tree at Forest Lake Resort proves time thrives in slow motion as it swallows a Public Telephone sign.**

# Arrival

Imagine a summer without fires. Nights warm, the forest takes in a visiting gust. Forest Lake Resort falls quiet after midnight. In the dance hall, the band packs away instruments, a world apart. Behind the bar, Jack Bliss, in black slacks, a white shirt, and suspenders, bottle-brushes the glasses. He pours a nightcap and chats with the last couple as they rise from their barstools. At the bar's end, Don Emerson—Forest Lake's owner, in brown khakis, loose print shirt, and wire-rimmed glasses—tallies receipts with a quiet smile. Blithe-as-summer youths sweep floors, and lights darken to a few amber silhouettes.

A couple makes a splashy bid goodnight and moseys to a cabin under pines, maples, and dogwoods. The memory of the night's music walks them home. Tuned by the music and the quieting of mental noise it provides, a litany of ease settles across the resort lands: stillness in the air, planets clustered among layers of stars, and barn owls hooting softly in faraway trees.

Within a mile or two of Forest Lake, a smorgasbord of resorts open their doors the next morning: Whispering Pines, Cobb Mountain Lodge, and Giffords (which later changed its name to Starview Lodge). In other quaint hollows and sunny spots of bountiful Cobb Mountain, Adams Springs, Pine Grove, Hobergs, Loch Lomond, Salmina's, Seigler's, and Harbin Hot Springs in Middletown complete the picture.

*****

In contrast to the turmoil of the late '60s, 1962 was a halcyon year. Families had nothing to do but enjoy the mountain retreat. The groups who stayed at Forest Lake's housekeeping cabins received meal tickets and free passes for The Lodge and most other activities. The bar cost a silver dollar or two, but the dance floor, pool, and the resort's own lake were included.[viii]

On the far left of The Lodge's first story, a curio shop sold decals and pine oddities: stopped clocks, little wooden treasure chests with brass adornments, tie racks for dad, trinkets of outhouses labeled, "Pointers" or "Setters," salt and pepper shakers, image-bottomed ash trays, and dreadful humor—polished plaques of a pregnant woman with the caption, "I Should Have Danced All Night." On the far right, The Lodge offered its own sprucing up area. A red-white-and-blue striped barber's pole turned out front; the shop inside was replete with newspapers, magazines, gels, and smells.

The elegant lodge, built in the early '30s[ix] by the hands of skillecraftspeople, boasted tear-drop siding and rows of picture windows that lent openness to The Lodge's serenity. Its uproarious quality resulted from the guests who arrived and wandered within its many environs and across its grounds.

The Forest Lake Lodge entrance was celebrated by two staircases that merged onto a generous landing in the middle and transformed into a grand set of stairs. Through the double doors, carloads entered the lobby, which featured a fireplace and circle of cushions where people gathered in the evenings.[x] They checked in at the counter where clean offices awaited and laughter erupted from the dining room around the corner.[xi] On the opposite side, the dance hall and the bar full of boisterous folks led to a cocktail lounge with smoky black and chrome tables and chairs. Sarah Huff,[xii] a slender cocktail hostess in her late forties with dark hair and glasses, took orders and ran back and forth to the bar.

The dance floor packed them in every night and carried the heat to dance under the spell to "Fever" and "So Rare." Frank Judnick, a very clean-cut man the youngsters called Mr. Frank, sported a trim mustache, a wry wit, and his requisite accordion. He extended a hardy handshake, welcoming guests. Host of the talent show, he backed the singers with ease. One young man wrote a song and performed it while Frank, with his ear leaning in, ran his hands across the keys, improvised a melody, and added a few kind words as the room applauded. He was the only man I was aware of—besides Mr. Rogers—who had a dynamic impact while interacting with youth. While Frank did not exude the same softness as the America icon and paragon of virtue, he certainly displayed the same level of kindness.

The prizes were in cash: a dollar for third place, two for second, and three for the toppermost.[xiii] Based mostly on popular choice and Frank's inner applause meter, the loot was handed out with a pat on the back and silver certificates, a legal tender circulated by the U.S. government. They used to call dollar bills greenbacks in those days, and they were redeemable for their face value in silver coins. Remarkably, from June '67 to June '68, they could be exchanged for raw silver bullion.[xiv]

Teenagers needed to earn walking-around money. It didn't fall from trees in my family, so I always looked for work. Since singing was as good as anything, I signed up for the talent show set up in front of the corner stage. My first time out, half way through it, I forgot the words to Johnny Horton's enormous hit song "Sink the Bismarck." Frank said, "Take a minute to remember." I said something like, "Ah shoot," into the mic. Frank joked, "Watch your language," and the room laughed. Then, with a compassionate tone: "Wait another moment; are you sure?" I nodded and slumped away.

The following week, determined to win, I rehearsed a number with a simpler structure, "Tom Dooley." As a 13-year-old, I must have struck the grownups as a bit unworldly for that folk ballad; however, I eked out each word, "Throughout history there have been many songs written about the eternal triangle…When the sun rises tomorrow, Tom Dooley must hang." After the ending phrase, "Poor boy, you're bound to die," I rolled into the pinball room with my three dollar prize. Later that evening, after guests had retreated to their rooms, my parents walked me into the bar. The bartender winked at my folks, handed me a bottle of champagne, and said, "You won first prize. Don't open it till you get home." Of course, my parents carried it out the front doors. Home safely in the cabin, the bottle trumpeted itself with a pop. My first cool sip of Napa champagne lasted till I slept.

After Mr. Frank concluded the talent show, the summer jazz band took the stage. It was fronted by a dream couple from The City: Billy Catalano,[xv] a debonair San Francisco native from a legendary musical family and his petite wife Arlene, the band's vocalist.[xvi] They played two or three sets a night while guests danced under the fractured light of the mirror ball. Folks were civil and mannerly on these floors—never a trace of trouble in the air. When the hot rods revved outside, no one inside seemed to notice. The hard guys who sometimes showed up with their sweatshirts turned inside out quickly got bored and hung around outside the doors of The Lodge to smoke Camels or Lucky Strikes.

Outside had more room for kids to talk about things like a father who died, an uncle who was shell-shocked by the war, or a mother who was drunk when they came home from school. The outside included those who had to grow up faster or got jobs younger than their friends because their family needed support. On back roads, outsiders growled like mountain lions in the moonlight as they talked about their dreams of a better life.

Inside, though, from the dance floor, we might enter the game room where a shy but newly successful songwriter played pinball. A pair of girls in pink and fuchsia pedal pushers wearing black Mary Janes would sidle up, watch flippers snap under the glass as it popped, clanged, rolled, rang, and all but chimed wedding bells. Songwriters got the girls back then, too.

We might venture again outdoors to the patio or drift through another door into the TV lounge. It sat empty except for the news or one of the few televised baseball games. In '62, the Giants won the pennant and the Yanks won the World Series after record rainouts in both cities delayed Game 6. In the stainless steel, porcelain tile kitchen down the hall, busy cooks Andy and Pete, wearing chef hats, darted among clatters of silver and sizzling grills and leaned over black-and-white stoves. Savory aromas drifted out back where the groundskeepers tended quaint outdoor patios. An evening group gathered for the party within the party. For fun, they watched high overhead as bats rolled their wings with wobbly radar precision in the rose-lavender twilight.

Folks seeking more fun ventured up the hill, past the resident fire engine (an at-the-ready, late '40s American LaFrance two-seater with polished ladder and waxed red paint[xvii]) to the open-air barn, where shuffleboard and ping-pong tables buzzed as patrons signed up to play. Ping-pong always had a long wait time. The long, sandy shuffleboard with its smooth, metallic pucks was less busy. To hang a puck at the far end was a once-in-a-lifetime gem. Like pitching a perfect game.

In the fall, the Cuban Missile Crisis took us to the brink of war with the Soviets. Thirteen days of waiting for the end of the world that fortunately did not happen. In 1962, Forest Lake's global backdrop was the atomic bomb. The resort provided plenty of cover for our fears, but still we carried them in bits of conversation.

On the dance floor, the fragrances broke loose, scattered with the tosses of the woodshop's sawdust. Couples and groups, fathers and daughters, mothers, sons, and cousins—everyone danced. They were captivated by the sheer beauty and sound of the summer jazz band. While the blissed-out piano player dropped in his harmonies, Arlene cast a sensual tone with her full, black hair and Billy counted each beat with the snap of his immaculate fingers before laying them on the mother-of-pearl valves of his trumpet. With his Italian movie star looks, Billy eyed her through the melody; singing and playing in time, their notes entwined. With the music building and blending, the trumpet reached for more. The drummer stirred the soup and the bass player hugged the beat. Arlene's eyes flared sapphire as she sang into the bundled pairs of dancers. In the crowd, the stage gazers desperately wished for her angel eyes to land on them.

The jazz band and the music, under the spotlights, made the players sweat as they poured on through the night. Double doors popped open near the band, and cool spells of air spilled in from the trees. When a mixed breeze rushed in with pine, oak, bay, and water from a nearby creek, pool, or lake, it brought the acclaimed clean air streaming across the summers of Cobb Mountain. The folks, drifting off to sleep in the nearby cabins, heard distant music swirling in their dreams.

# La Sequía

Nubes estelares caen en cascada sobre la vieja casa de montaña,
el fuego tararea, la chimenea crepita, mi espalda está contra la llama.
Hoy—un día primaveral en diciembre—
plantando narcisos al final del sol bajo.

Ni una gota de lluvia ha caído este otoño,
aunque algunas cayeron hace rato—sin sonido.

Pues, son preocupaciones, éstas sobre la sequía.
No obstante, debo decir, aun podemos sumergirnos
hondamente en las aguas minerales.
Arroyos fríos y fuentes termales corren en la colina escarpada,
esta cordillera del condado de Lake, salpicada
con pino ponderosa, roble, laurel, y abeto.
Habrá pavor este verano si no tenemos lluvia.

Los condados de California se preparan para la congelación,
otra mañana de escarcha y sol
sin ninguna nube solitaria, día tras día.
Sin embargo, no puedo evitar preguntarme,
¿por qué es primavera en diciembre?

Sembraré una cama de narcisos por el rehilete de tu jardín,
ya que estos días veo el rayo de luz más amarillo en el sol dorado,
calentando la tierra ya abrasadora.
Sin ninguna preocupación de una temporada, eventualmente, de sequía.

A mi parecer, no estaría mal orar o bailar o soñar con tormentas
y estados de ánimo que cobran vida por el poder de un sueño.
Y que tú y yo corriéramos bajo las tormentas más salvajes y húmedas
en la historia de California, llenando lagos, pozos, corrientes, embalses,
fregaderos de cocina y, sí—piscinas.

No me molestaría un día nubloso
donde el mundo sacude el cambio que esperamos;
mañana, anhelo escuchar el Arroyo Seco cantar
y el cielo oscuro con la llamada del trueno.

*. . no estaría mal orar o bailar o soñar con tormentas*
*. y estados de ánimo que cobran vida por el poder de un sueño—de lluvia.*

# Drought

Star clouds cascade over the old mountain home,
fire hums, flue's crackling, my back's against the flame.
Today—a spring day in December—
planting daffodils at the finale of the low sun.

Not a drop of rain has fallen this fall,
yet a few fell a while ago—without a sound.

No, they're a worry of a thought, these about drought.
Though I must say, we can still soak low in hot mineral waters.
Cold creeks and hot springs run on the rugged hill,
this Lake County Ponderosa-Oak-Bay-and-Fir-studded range.
There'll be a day of dread this summer if we don't get any rain.

The counties of California brace for the freeze,
another morn' of frost and sun
without a lonely cloud, day after day.
Yet I cannot help but wonder, why is it spring in December?

I'll plant a bed of daffodils by your garden windmill,
as these days I see the yellowest light splinter in the golden sun,
warming the already sweltering earth.
Without a worry of a time, by and by, of a drought.

As I see it, it wouldn't hurt to pray or dance or dream of rainstorms
and moods brought to life by the power of a dream.
And that you and I would run through the wildest and wettest
rainstorms in California's history, filling the lakes, wells, streams, reservoirs,
kitchen sinks and, yeah—swimming pools.

I wouldn't mind a cloudy day
where the world shakes the change we hope for;
tomorrow, I long to hear Dry Creek singing
and the sky growing dark with thunder calling.

*. . . it wouldn't hurt to pray or dance or dream of rainstorms*
*and moods brought to life by the power of a dream—of rain.*

# Horse Trails on the Edge of Shangri La

A short walk from the Forest Lake housekeeping cabins, a robust horse corral—built out of pine rails and round redwood posts—held a dozen slow horses on the current site of the Cobb Village Inn. On walks home from the resort, I would stop, lean on the rails, and watch them snooze. I didn't know anything about horses but was drawn to them by some subconscious detection of ancient harmony. Western movies and television episodes like *Spin and Marty* or shows like *Maverick*—popular in the late '50s and early '60s—also made the corral feel like a homeland found a hundred years from home.

Jim Salmina ran the horses at Forest Lake and Hoberg's. Craig Newfield and his sister, Linda, ran the trail rides at Forest Lake. One evening, a stable hand in worn harness boots, blue plaid, and hat ambled to the rail and asked my name. He said he had seen me hanging around the corral. Like an older brother, he said, "If you ever want to pitch in, come by early and I'll show you a few things." I woke up at dawn the next day and showed up to see silhouettes of horses peering into the darkness.

First, I learned to cinch up a saddle. "They may puff out their ribs, so you have to wait a few minutes and adjust it again or the saddle will be too loose. Horses are tricky, but these ones here are pretty good," he said. After that, I helped the brother and sister team lead the horses out to Forest Lake Drive. My world of beautiful notions had become a reality. The Newfields and the folks who gathered around them—trustworthy people who treated others fairly—inspired me to do my best.

I learned to work with the customers and showed them how to mount from the left and slide the balls of their feet into the stirrups without hooking their heels. When enough riders showed up, a line of geldings and mares clip-clopped into the resort past the pool crowd, who smiled and waved. At the lake, where blue dragonflies buzzed and the call and response of frogs sang, we watched the drifting boats and heard the voices of people relishing the day.

After the lake walk, the route wound around the south side of the resort up the steep trail. The modest train of steeds panted, heaved, and bolstered the climb with their hind legs to reach for higher ground. "Lean forward," hollered the leader. Up that narrow canyon trail we rode; the horses blew charges of air through their wet nostrils and pushed on—never wilting from the load they bore on their backs. With anxious eyes, riders sat in their saddles and watched as hooves pounded dust, listened as lungs huffed and wheezed, and smelled the sweat that grew in patches on their own mounts' necks.

Once the team reached the peak and descended the hill, looking down into rocks and trees below was a bit unnerving as the trail narrowed. "Lean back," yelled the man up front. "Easy does it." Some patted them on the rump to show gratitude for their courage. A few riders listened to the aging but sure-footed ones who, with every step, encouraged us to be aware of the moment. Good trail horses paced those narrow trails with a serenity drenched in history. Those quiet horses were practiced in the art of survival like true descendants of the 15th century Andalusian breed, who outlived centuries of war and hunger and—for a long hour—relieved our everyday worries. They didn't want to tumble into a ravine, either. Riding the trail around the resort wasn't exactly tightrope walking in those days, but if anyone leaned too far sideways, it would have been scary. Fortunately, that never occurred; though the riders held the reins, the horses knew the way.

Back at the hitching post, the customers wandered back to the resort and I cleaned the horses' hooves. One of the stable hands taught me how. "First, let them know you are standing there by a pat on the rump so they don't get spooked. Don't grab the hoof but slide down your hand from the thigh and—with your body—lightly push the horse's weight over to the opposite leg. Then, you lift the hoof as if you're asking permission. Once in hand, clean the crud with this hoof pick." I was handed a tool about six inches long that was bent ninety degrees at the top and had a pointed end. "Do not hit the frog[xviii] with the sharp end. The horse won't like it."

Across the road from the horse corral, at the corner of Golf Road and 175, lay the sixth green of a pristine golf course. (Those years, as long as The Pro, George "Twitch" Twitchell, didn't catch us, it was the place for kids to sell golf balls we dug out of the drink—or out of the creek—on the fifth hole.) Under the mountain backdrop of a tree-lifted sky, the deep green fairways were a serene challenge rather than grueling. The golf course was a delight to play. As intact as a preserved 1950s postcard, marbled somewhat by time, the open space turned into a Cobb treasure. Players crossed a bridge over the creek in at least two settings; robins gathered in droves along the fairways before and after rains and when the Rain Birds[xix] sprayed water.

Jones Creek, where rainbow trout hid between rocks in white water, ran behind the ninth green near Golf Road. The creek, rushing or idling in pools, sang past blackberry vines, bays, and pine roots; it purred along banks imbedded with stones on the long sixth fairway, rolled and surged past the fifth and third holes, and disappeared.

In the bustling "Country Club" years, pairs and foursomes of players turned up every hour on long summer days. Carts and caddies were available by reservation. It was another place where kids earned a few dollars. Often the better the player, the bigger the tip. Even so, that wasn't the case one Saturday afternoon sometime around '62: The Pro, Twitch, tipped the paltry amount of a buck and a quarter for the whole day. But that was okay; most teenagers and some adults, too, would have caddied for free.

Stu Miller, the fabled Giants relief pitcher, played two rounds of nine holes each. A mild-mannered gentleman in slacks and a light shirt, he stood about the size of Robert Kennedy. Easy to talk to, he preferred being addressed by his first name. "Nobody calls me Mr. Miller," he said one Saturday morning, far away from Candlestick Park and its wind-swept pitching mound. Stu and his partner Mr. Santos, who never spoke except for hello and goodbye, played error-free rounds, and Stu signed his scorecards, which have been lost over time. Later that night, my father surmised from Mr. Santos' strong, quiet bearing that he was Hall of Famer Ron Santo of the Chicago Cubs. Nevertheless, that was never proven, and we dropped the claim in the name of Mars, horseplay, and a few cold Burgermeister beers.

I'm not sure what year George Hoberg, Jr., took over the golf course, bar, and restaurant, but they prospered under his work ethic and leadership for many years. He served tables, tended bar, and was a family favorite for decades—a reserved man unless diners engaged him, as they always did. He'd dash a smile and be off to the nearest table, listening more than talking, always with a sense of humor. Taller than my other heroes, Robert Kennedy, whom I'd stood face to face with at USF in 1968, and Stu Miller, George's golf handicap was a modest two. Or was it four? His golf form seemed akin to his management style: quiet, sleek, and professional. In his golf swing, his body arced, and his hands landed back over his shoulder. Golf seemed a time of solitude for George Hoberg, Jr. I watched him—a silent presence on the course in the odd hours of early morning and evening. Apart from his role as the dean of Cobb golf's flourishing years, he was out on the fairways, studying and practicing each shot to improve his game. In a dim morning fog at the third tee, he'd take that graceful swing and then disappear onto the fairway as he followed the ball to the green. Once he arrived, you might say he was putting into the streaking night sky.

Four of Forest Lake's bathing beauties: Grace, Marlene, my mother Muriel, and Mrs. Cain in the early 1960s. A few summers earlier, after a round of gin fizzes, my parents happened upon a lot between two creeks on High Road near Forest Lake, fell in love with the property, and made an offer on the spot. Years later, my parents completed construction of their first cabin in 1962, before this photo was taken.

# Angel Eyes, What'll I Do?

The late '50s and early '60s were the age of Don Emerson, a quiet and studious gentleman who owned and managed Forest Lake during its prosperous years. Later, a partnership developed between the ebullient Joe Breen and the slender Vic Tamera who, despite his occasional hot temper, looked frail and appeared introverted. On the other hand, Joe relaxed at the pool every day and engaged anybody willing to enjoy his company. And many did just that. He was deeply bronzed by sunshine and heavily bathed in sun cream. Vic's son—my friend Vincent—was more like Joe Breen, portly and gregarious. Massed with sculpted black hair, Vincent befriended everybody and danced with ladies of all ages. [xx]

That group kept Forest Lake vibrant and thriving until popular tastes and changing times lured families to more exotic escapes and resorts became endangered relics of a lost romantic era. Forest Lake was sold for its water[xxi] at the end of the '60s to Boon Lodge and Tom (Sully) Sullivan. They bought their bottling gear from none other than renowned Perrier Water. Boon and Sully developed the Forest Lake and Cobb Mountain Water brands early in the spring water business. When the industry became lucrative and competitive, they finally sold to Nestle®, who continued to bottle its spring water. It is now privately owned.

Forest Lake may be remembered by many, but then again, by few or none. Certainly, though, resort guests will recall the evenings of jazz. They swayed long into the night, soaking up summer ease. The music felt so close, so full of alpine air and pine aroma, that its presence drifted into conversations, such as lyrics from "Angel Eyes" and "What'll I Do?" The room listened to "Blue Moon" and danced as pools of colorful light drifted across the bandstand. All that wasn't enough to save its ultimate decline; the resort era died.

Another casualty of that era was Hoberg's. In 1974, Maharishi Mahesh Yogi, an Indian guru famous for creating Transcendental Meditation and his association with The Beatles, purchased Hoberg's Resort and its grounds. His proverb was, "The natural tendency of the mind is to seek greater happiness." Hoberg's itself was a place archived with families seeking greater happiness, if only for a week in summer. As a symbolic notion, it looked like a good fit—Hoberg's and meditation. Yet it wasn't open to the public. No longer were the resort grounds and historical structures an inviting place to stop for coffee and breakfast, like the Loch Lomond Road House had been for many years. It wasn't the Hoberg's we knew and loved except for lonely drives past. It was in a separate world of its own; most of us longed for its return—at least those I talked to. Underutilized by Maharishi International University members, Hoberg's faded into its neglected grounds and was nearly abandoned for ten years. Finally, it sold to investors in 2010.[xxii] The investors' idea was to bring back its former brilliance. Restoration was underway; the dream died the day the Valley Fire bombed it to ruins.

But in the glory days—those romantic Cobb Mountain glory days—the only road past Forest Lake Resort was the road through it. For many years, the larger road past it didn't exist. Traffic wasn't "traffic" but a purple onion Plymouth, a cream and green Ranch Wagon, a black and chrome '49 Ford, and a heavenly blue '62 Impala. The cars unloaded four or six people at a time. Station wagons of all sizes, colors, and shapes drove in and parked at the curb by the pool.

News of the world drifted up from the valleys and towns with the arriving carloads. Word of mouth swept through the resort, mingling with TV news and radios with lousy reception. There was a sense of otherworldliness though; and at the same time, it seemed a perfect world, a summer for anyone to enjoy. The news let us know there was trouble outside the invisible gates of the Cobb Mountain resorts. Even so, we didn't shoot messengers or fire the envoys back then. We lived with the atom bomb, and the enemy was always the Soviet Union. Memories of World War II, Nazi Germany, and The Bomb were spoken in whispers at the bar. A number of the guys were veterans who had empathy for the people they liberated and little mercy for Hitler or fascism. Freedom was the passion of the land.

At The Fountain, bells rang in the pinball machines. Kids formed new friendships and ran free of most parental rules except the basics of eating and sleeping. Some vied to work behind the counter for little pay, a free hot dog, and a tip. If they could make a shake and talk to people, they stuck. Manners were a must. The affable ladies who worked behind the counter handed out quarters for the juke box, usually requesting their own favorite songs. These may have been "Love Me Tender" or "Break It To Me Gently." "Ramblin' Rose" resounded everywhere.

We learned later how troubled things were in other places as we inched towards the pivotal year of 1968. Far away across America, a swimming pool in Baltimore, Maryland, became the place for a racial battle in the summer of 1962.[xxiii] An 11 year old boy named Elijah Cummings[xxiv] was led from a pool to safety from a racist mob by Juanita Jackson Mitchell,[xxv] a teacher, along with another dozen black children. To put that event into a Cobb Mountain setting would seem improbable, yet its likelihood in America has become shockingly revealed in recorded history.

Here, the bronze-tanned lifeguard never had to save anyone from drowning or lead kids from the pool to safety. The world of trouble seemed as far away as the copper penny dives, rolls of black-and-white dice, late night dancing, swim races, hayrides, and kids running free seem to us in our tech-crazed culture.

Forest Lake was a dreamer's door cracked open to a vast American Dream. Decades later, a smaller number of resorts continue to provide a temporary respite from technology, traffic, and work, where we see through the crack into the less complex world of imagination and possibility. That world still reserves space in Lake County's Harbin Hot Springs, a retreat center, in Middletown. Simply called Harbin by locals, it is world-famous for opening the "doors of perception"[xxvi] for guests who seek its sanctuary. Destroyed by the Valley Fire, it reopened its spring-fed pools for day use on January 16, 2019. Its mineral waters continue to flow under the centuries of fires that have come and gone and will come back again, as nature intends.

Cobb Mountain and its friends and neighbors in Middletown still share golden-era hospitality: Hardester's, Cobb Mountain Pizza, Mountain High, the Post Office, Cobb Pacific, and a neighborly array of shops at Loch Lomond. Middletown has Star Gardens, Cowpoke Cafe, Lovie's Garden Supply, Community Farmer's Market, Hardester's Market & Hardware, B&G Tire, and many more. Middletown's service standard is as welcoming as Cobb's; they value the lost art of casual production, and their subtle gestures of appreciation to their customers are rare finds in larger cities where such civility is often lost.

**Painting by Cobb Mountain artist, Wayne Darby, R.I.P.**
Darby frequented Starview and was a friend of my father. He painted
Cobb's plentiful mountains and valleys. They bring back the scent of pine
and the clear air for which Cobb is known. In this one, you can almost hear
the Acorn Woodpeckers hammering in the trees. His paintings, in the large
halls of lodges and spacious rooms that are of Lake County's original
character, depict a generation's perspective. A simple place or scene
endures most when it is showcased in a location appreciated by an artist's
persistent attention.

## Ojos de Paseantes

Estando allí todos esos años como vecinos,
a través de más de un aguacero, día de sequía, y peligro de incendio,
los árboles discutieron las cosas.
Cuando una ráfaga del *Arroyo Seco* los despertó,
se apresuraron a que los ojos de los paseantes notaran
algo en el otro mundo,
tan real como un cúmulo de nubes de verano.

Ve a la deriva como puedas mientras las nubes, también, discutan las cosas,
vibrantes en el más allá que aterriza en la poesía o la canción que
elijas perseguir con la multitud de alas
en la parte más alta del cielo,
enmendando el dolor por los perdidos árboles sagrados.

**The once thriving shady grove became a hollow of scorched
trees that were eventually felled and split into firewood.**

## Passerbys' Eyes

Standing by all those years as neighbors,
through many a downpour, drought day, and fire danger,
the trees talked things over.
When *Dry Creek's* wafts awoke them,
they hastened the passerbys' eyes to notice
something in the other world,
real as the wisp of summer clouds.

Drift as you will while the clouds, too, talk things over,
vibrant in the afterlife that lands in the poem or song
you choose to chase with the multitudes of wings
into the higher side of the sky,
mending grief for the lost, sacred trees.

**Two views of Dry Creek Road (above and on opposite page) after the Valley Fire. As illustrated in the photo opposite, an important part of California's native beauty—canopies of oak trees and their shadowed light streaming across its roads—has been lost.**

# Linger Long Those Lake Sounds

In the 1950s, at The Forest Lake Fountain and across the road, the bar of the elegant lodge, as well as in every café, bar, and resort on Cobb Mountain, records played anytime nickel and silver rolled into jukeboxes. Walking up to a jukebox was like walking into a luminous library of musical wonder and awe; they ensnared the imagination like a leap to San Francisco's "Playland at the Beach" on a hot day. Those magnificent machines were YouTube for a dime, installed in Elvis's Cadillac. "I Can't Stop Loving You" by Ray Charles and "The Loco-Motion" by Little Eva carried the moods, as did "Duke of Earl" by Gene Chandler and "Blue Monday" by Fats Domino. The Drifters and Connie Francis always cast a spell. "The Twist" started a dance that generations would sample like the Hula Hoop.

Fast forward to 2021 (and beyond) and picture a pair of ancient oak trees shading Forest Lake Resort's empty main drive. One tree devours the "Public Telephone" sign, the bench in between hauled away long ago. In the resort days, it was a preferred place to meet friends and to stand around on warm nights or curious afternoons watching, talking, and fooling around until getting hungry. Wanting some "pickins," kids fled to The Fountain, ordered baskets of hot dogs, burgers, and fries, playing those old time songs. Some approached the jukebox as a place of study while the new records rolled out of the red striped Seeburg Select-o-matic. "I'm Sorry" and "Only the Lonely" circled and spun 'round after ballads by Marty Robbins, treasured story-songs (also called saga songs) by Johnny Horton, and Motown hits filled The Fountain walls with sound. The song that rekindled folk music, "Tom Dooley," caught on; the solo[xxvii] of Del Shannon's "Runaway" pierced the twilight zone and still lives there.

Those records undoubtedly had locomotion—they are forever savored in our senses and hearts. We blur the boundaries of time while listening to them; they are a soundtrack for time itself. They played at the crux and resounded from our age-old crossroads: the intersection of rhythm and melody held decades that ran together in one vibrating musical experience.

Although those years have come and gone, this tranquil setting still lingers in the memories of folks who have stayed at Forest Lake Resort. Music evolved; and in 1964, the British Invasion landed in our living rooms with a different take on our own American dreams. Jazz took a back seat to songs like, "Gloria" (Them, Van Morrison's band from Belfast, Northern Ireland), "House of the Rising Sun" (The Animals), and "She Loves You" (The Beatles). Tracks from *Meet the Beatles!* and The Rolling Stone's *Out of Our Heads* blasted from car radios; most notably, "(I Can't Get No) Satisfaction" rang out in back-road convertibles all over the mountain. As the generations kept growing and the music kept changing, '60s music took the world by the throat. Yet the jazz of Billy and Arlene Catalano never left our hearts. How could it? We heard it, walked with its rhythmic step, and heard the voicings of its instruments—up close or through the trees—everywhere we walked in the Forest Lake nightscape.

Now, past the running creek and gray pews of Our Lady of the Pines, where quails' wings flutter towards blackberries, Forest Lake and its tiny island idle in neglect. Still, waterfowl gather there on short afternoons; and on a few dim winter days, the lake freezes over. Back in '62, the year my family built "the cabin that started it all,"[xxviii] a stocky wooden dock and a half-dozen faded turquoise, mustard, and pink rowboats dozed and bobbed on the lake—its aura sparkled in radiant sun-blue diamonds.

29

Forest Lake now sits abandoned, deep green and shadowed, crying out for restoration. Not every town has a lake full of summer dreams. The relationship of time and space is evident in the landscape; I imagine the world's lost romantics paddling past the island of pine and brush, where mallards played hide-and-go-seek until dark, drifting into the tules and reeds, and dissolving into the night.

The boats were finally taken away after their last summer, sometime in the '70s; the dock lay open at the lake's edge for no other purpose than to support fisherpeople and dock-seekers. It was an ideal spot to seek solitude or to take a friend who'd never been there before. We would sit on folded legs like Zen students, light up Marlboros, and watch the water and the island for signs of life, a flicker of wings overhead. Sometimes a line of poetry would come to mind: "I heard the old, old men say, 'all that's beautiful drifts away, like the waters.'"[xxix]

Night. Air. The lake remembers the slow, walking feet. Chance pairs of young philosophers, under the spell of celestial awakenings, pondered ideas in those rarest-of-night walks. If I could ransack time, shake up passivity, and raise thousands of dollars for a good cause, it would be for the lake's restoration.

The gorgeous and vivid trumpet of Billy Catalano soared at dusk one last time as it passed through red leather doors into history. Over the dice cups pounding on the smoke-ringed bar, between sips of bourbon and maraschino cherries, the trumpet fell silent in a forest emptied of guests. Yet the families who wound their way up Highway 175 without blowing a tire, burning up a clutch, or boiling over a radiator now rely on memories and keepsakes from friends and neighbors because their own artifacts burned up. Folks seek the company of pictures, stories, and tales of the resort days and the music that flourished from the different views of celestial nightscapes. *Visit Kelseyville* and *Cobb Mountain Area Historical Society* are but two Facebook groups that share photos and personal and historical accounts of Lake County resorts.

After the resort era's heyday had ended and Forest Lake had sold, the new owners followed the tradition that began way back in the '20s with Calso Water®, whose corporate entity began in 1945 by bottling locally sourced mineral water.[xxx] On the renowned grounds of this historic place, a new Forest Lake supported the production of its most precious resource: the spring water that rushes from its own rocky soil. The wooded property, its springs, and structures outlived the Valley Fire. The Lodge—along with folks' memories from the heart of "America's Switzerland"—still stands in Lake County, California.

## Oda a una Bombera Voluntaria —*para Gary Grutkowski*
## El Incendio de Wilbur Hot Springs

Quisiera ser una bombera
en San Francisco en 1906, o ahora, hoy,
en los lugares donde
buscamos entre las cenizas.

Quisiera ser una bombera
en Wilbur Hot Springs en 2014,
cuando los dragones destrozaron las
ventanas y devoraron el hotel *grande dame*.

Hermoso. Encantador. Peligroso.
El fuego dorado asciende, día y noche.
Pase lo que pase, el incendio continúa.

Quisiera ser una bombera
este verano en los condados remotos
de California,
donde en los pastos furiosos
trabajaría el agua.

Derramarlo, empapar la tierra quemada,
calmar el terror, ahogar el hedor y el miedo.

Quisiera andar en camiones de bomberos,
salvando autobuses escolares llenos de estudiantes
en el camino a Humboldt.
Jóvenes de ojos inocentes dejando el hogar para siempre,
sueños familiares rotos, fragmentados por el fuego.

Rabia y belleza. Terror en llamas. Reunir, huir, y esperar.

Quisiera ser una bombera
que pudiera flotar en agua profunda,
ojos hacia el cielo, mirando los cuervos volar
a su árbol de morada nocturna, camiones a la espera.

# *Ode to a Volunteer Firefighter*—*for Gary Grutkowski*
## *Wilbur Hot Springs Fire*

I wish I were a fireman
in San Francisco in 1906, or now, today,
in the places where
we sift through the ashes.

I wish I were a firefighter
at Wilbur Hot Springs in 2014,
when dragons shattered windows
and devoured the *grande dame* hotel.

Beautiful. Lovely. Dangerous.
The golden fire rises, day and night.
No matter what, fire goes on.

I wish I were a fireman
this summer in the remote counties
of California,
where in the raging grasses
I would work the water.

Pour it out, drench the scorched ground,
calm the terror, drown out stench and fear.

I wish I could ride on fire trucks,
saving school buses of students
on their way to Humboldt.
Doe-eyed youth leaving home forever,
family dreams broken, fragmented by fire.

Rage and beauty. Terror aflame. Gather, flee, and wait.

I wish I were a firefighter
that I might float in deep water,
eyes to the sky, watching crows fly for night's home tree,
trucks at the ready.

Enter Starview's open gates and its nearly
tropical setting on Cobb Mountain.

# Figure on the Road
## Valley Fire

She spent her nights under the moonlight as regulars laughed, drank, and talked 'til closing time at Starview Lodge. Then one night, the fire stormed in, the moon vanished, and the next day, ways of lives smoldered, towers of smoke rose, and the figure on the road was suddenly alone. The few things standing were a chimney of stone, the scorched torches of many trees, a pool with boiled water at the bottom, and a handmade barbecue of block and metal.

Behind the figure on the road was the Tiki Lounge, a summer place of laughter, argument, and affection—now in stark ruins. Before her eyes once stood the legendary Starview Lodge. Its grand, simple design included a stone fireplace, blue windows, wood shingles, a hospitable bar, and pine booths in a scarlet-draped dining room. In cold winters, neighbors and veterans walked along pathways to the front door. Once inside, they strolled past the fireplace, palms down over flames, where whole logs and half-truths burned through the night. Sparks caught their bare hands or arced like fireflies to the blackened stone and mortar. There stood the long bar with red leather stools, its cobalt blue infused windows, a pool room, and copious glasses; now and then, you got a free drink if you sang. All at the Starview Lodge.

Then, the music in the room leapt about louder, as did the thunderous roar when steaming food arrived at dining room tables. The blue windows shone like sapphire, and when the trees breathed loudly—a close distance, a breath away at night—in the tall winds outside, the crew closed the ruby velvet drapes. Recovered by Van from the Fox Theater in San Francisco, they lent the room a warm, soft tone.

After our fill of food and platter-chatter, generations in threes or fours stopped at the hearth-and-fire and arms landed on shoulders. Shout-outs clamored for Van, Rick, and Barbara and the bar folk: throaty jokes and belly-loud hollers followed fathers and sons, daughters and mothers back into the night.

The figure's saddened, melted face revealed that she was alone with the Valley Fire and alone with the rising, choking, and smoldering empty remains that followed. Every soul fled where she stands now; no deer, raven, red-tailed hawk, quail, tree squirrel, lizard, or snake remained. Cars full of friends and families, loners, walk-ins, and delivery truck drivers escaped with their lives. Only disfigured trees remained, bark burned clean without leaf or pine needle. The lost laughter and loneliness of twilight seemed as ancient as the sculpture in the fountain, where children and guests had splashed at her feet on summer days.

Folks who sat at the bar or relaxed around the pool's piano-key tile, ate Van and Rick's grilled ribs and spit-roasted feasts, and drank Barbara's companionable pours will never forget that fountain standing in the bathing pool. It stood through the combustion of the forest and village outside that homespun lodge, high up on Cobb Mountain's winding roads. The years' worth of work it would take to grind the road clear of the fire's massive exhalation began. The figure on the road survived it all, an icon of our own existence.

**Three generations: Timothy, Casey, and Robert Williams
enjoy the Tiki Lounge on a beautiful day at Starview Lodge.**

Starview before and after; the fireplace
stood on the left, inside the front door.

The Tiki Lounge, wading pool, and the figure on the road.

The Hoberg's sign was a lone survivor of the 2015 Valley Fire.
The land became a logger's site, and the wood was given away.

# On the Deep Bronze Strings of the Sun
## Valley Fire

They call it the other side of the mountain,
where tree stumps smolder through the night and the red sun rises.
The Valley Fire has raged past, the Cobb Village unbroken.
Neighborhoods and hamlets lie in curls of toxic smoke.

The occupied streets, strange as shock waves.
The flames' dragooning laugh, its million cackles clashing
in broad sweeps into its own hideout, deep within our hearts,
where clouds dance and joy swims—
when we kick the firestorm back out the door.

We have seen the fire destroy its own path,
create the furthering of its own twisted soul;
a trespasser without conscience, a thief of our shattered senses.

It ended decades of celebrated summers
around the mountain roads of history,
through the trees, on decks, in many homes and cabins.

It obliterated a restoration-in-progress of Cobb's celebrated stage stop
at Hoberg's Resort, where families swam in water drawn from the spring
and felicity hummed along while the music played …
on the deep bronze strings of the sun.

**The Pine Grove sign welcomes guests
to enjoy life on Cobb Mountain.**

# Winds Cross a Field of Dreams
## Valley Fire

Loch Lomond, a wooded hideaway with 420 residents once called Little Italy, is Cobb's surviving northern stalwart of a resort village, complete with mail service and a grocery, coffeeshop, fire station, and roadhouse. When the first photo of Loch Lomond appeared on the Facebook group, *Friends of Cobb Mountain*, a dead weight lifted from our fire vigil and one long, sleepless night was over. Something at Cobb had survived. Still, we had to soldier on through the endless news reports.

Nonetheless, we had caught a break: we received direct news from a voice familiar to most Cobb residents, Robert Stark—the water company manager for decades. He wrote "Fire Reports," which he posted after the inferno began. He provided details. A hungry journalist, he gathered observations, wrote, and reported them all—the damages and the parts of neighborhoods that survived. *Friends of Cobb Mountain* also gave survivors a place to share their grief, losses, and the many conflicting emotions and problems after the fire.

Soon after, on September 15, 2015, two more Facebook groups sprang into action: *Cobb Mountain Rising* and *Cobb Friends and Family*. Communication about everything under the Cobb sun, moon, and stars still flourishes daily in these groups. When a mountain lion wanders on quiet feet out of the forest into a neighborhood, we read about it. When we need local news about things like upcoming council meetings and food giveaways during the pandemic, we find out about it from these groups.

Fortunately, the Valley Fire never penetrated the intensely dense area of Pine Grove's furthest western flank. Thus, Pine Grove was spared the fate of Hoberg's, Starview, Anderson Springs, Harbin, and—from decades earlier—the tragic ends of magnificent Adams Springs, Cobb Mountain Lodge, and many others.[xxxi]

In my earliest Cobb memory, I was asleep on the floor of an army tent at Pine Grove Resort in 1953. I woke up screaming; my parents' argument was so thunderous that it shook the tent next to us as well. I still remember words that don't bear repeating, yet things got better as time passed. Pine Grove Resort relaxed the fighting reflexes of my father, Robert Williams, a World War II veteran, and my mother Muriel, who was orphaned and self-supporting from the age of 16.

Throughout the '50s, the Williams blended family of five had rented cabins in Pine Grove. We stayed in places owned by Walsh and by Dooley (originally spelled differently), in the neighborhood off Rainbow Drive, spending our evenings at bingo in the dance hall. Walking back to those cabins with flashlights in pitch darkness except for a bright moon, constellations, and clusters of stars, we wondered how much light we could borrow from the night sky. The ground evolved into a musical landscape: the call and response of crickets and frogs. Venus, as big as an apple, stood out among the multitudes of glowing *estrellas,*[xxxii] flung, scattered, and brilliant. Her radiance of melting silver poured light into our imaginations and onto the path. It seemed a time when the eyes of the world were full of beautiful landscapes. After my brothers relocated to faraway places, our dwindling family returned to Cobb Mountain for decades, making many lifelong friends there.

Nothing could be better than summer on Cobb Mountain! A walk to the pool. Sounds of laughter and splashing. Bingo cards with bean markers. The quiet tension anticipating the next number. Sweet smells of taffy and licorice flooding the air. Ah, summer fragrance healing all battles. Under the pines, the warmth of others, the companionship of the natural world: infinite shades of blue sky, clear-speaking streams, and coveys of valley quail dashing into lavish blackberry vines.

The swimming pool, like a frozen lake in winter, was ice cold—no doubt about it—and that was its allure. To swim was to dare and endure. In other pools, people swam for pleasure. Here, though, you had to swim in the cold water drawn from a mountain stream and challenge the elements of this mystifying universe without shivering to death.

The main store of midnight green welcomed customers as kinfolk and offered the inviting space of a café with its stools, counter, cream-and-green milkshake machines, and virtuous greetings. The grill's delicious aromas of bacon and onions invited us to stay. The jukebox, which played country and western sounds like Patsy Cline, also spun honey-gold Sun 45s of Johnny Cash and Jerry Lee Lewis. After filling up with food and drink, we would play catch on the softball diamond, a rugged field where the backstop backed up to Bottle Rock—a short walk from the store. At Pine Grove, getting to the next spot required only a short walk. Cars rarely shifted out of park.

In the '60s, the earliest days of the British Invasion, word got around that a band playing Beatles songs was coming to Pine Grove. Throngs of youths showed up, a few parents stood with wide eyes, and some of the older siblings were drawn in. More folks crowded in, it seemed, than movie night and bingo combined—something new was happening. The band lined up as a four-piece outside the main hall and sang in full harmony: "Please Please Me," "This Boy," "Chains," "All My Loving," and many more, trading guitar parts and vocals.

45

Undoubtedly, this first night, long before the term "cover band" came into usage, hundreds of kids heard Beatles songs played live while delirious with sweat, sharing the love with a newfound friend at their side. After that night, the talk among inspired kids included findings from newspaper searches, hitching rides to the few music stores that existed, and even taking the bus to San Francisco pawn shops to pick out a guitar and take it home. One such carousing youth may have been international blues guitarist Chris Cain. As a young man, he spent days practicing the accordion and guitar in the Cain family cabin, looking east from Bottle Rock Road towards the Circle-of-Life Loop, where creeks gush around ferns, watercress, and moss-covered stones into Cobb Village.

Sometime after that, Pine Grove added a second pool. In the '80s, the resort was still going strong, and it provided pools and cabins just as it had two decades earlier. Wanting the full circle experience late one summer day, my young son Casey and I joined the honey bees and gathered the day's last sunlight to take in the pools. He swam with neon water wings, and a guy at the pool suggested he wouldn't need them next spring. The following April, Casey wiggled out of those water wings and swam freely; a dozen years later, he started his own full circle experience with his son, Bailey Williams, in Sonoma County. In this case, the poet's son became a comedian, and his son became a community college student and university track prospect for San Francisco State University.

Pine Grove remains high on many lists of favorite places. I stopped by in the '90s and swam in the cold pool with a contemplative friend. The cold water felt meditative; it seemed akin to Kabuki Springs & Spa in San Francisco's Japantown—still, quiet, and reflective. I watched my friend open her eyes under the water and pull herself up from the pool's light-blue layers to sit at its edge.

Even after the end of the resort era, a few resorts—especially Pine Grove—still enjoy the tradition of providing cabins and pools for family vacations. The desperate question is, will they continue to regenerate, or will their ashes become a monument to the venomous Valley Fire?

*****

As we split downed trees for firewood one cool morning, Paul, my retired neighbor, talks about his parents and grandparents spending summers at Pine Grove dating back to the early 1900s. On many a hot day in the '60s, he and his brothers sloshed through the creek from Pine Grove all the way to the lake. On those adventures, they'd wade where the still waters ran[xxxiii] and the trout swam. The deep pool in Jones Creek, behind the real estate office, was their high-water mark. They waded up to their necks. In the '60s, the office was once a sought-after breakfast and lunch spot where customers lined up outside to get a table. Across from the now abandoned pub, it drew many patrons there to watch the creek for rainbow trout idling in magnificence and in plain sight.

As the morning climbs, we roll a log to the splitter and stop for Coke. Paul shows me the damage beetles do to pine trees in a drought. A split log, lying open in the sunlight, the color of straw, looks like a save-for-winter treasure. A water channel, the color of a blood bay horse, runs through the log's core. Pale forms of caterpillar-like larvae lay squeezed into its channels. "You see how they plant themselves in the water channel," he says. "The tree dies of thirst."

In such a wooded place as this, it's refreshing to speak in generational language. Other times, it becomes gut-wrenching as we uncover rock-solid details of our World War II heroes and impactful events of the war. My teenaged father spent his summers with the U.S.

47

Army's 71<sup>st</sup> Infantry Division that landed in France's Port of Le Havre. The point where the Seine River meets the English Channel in the Normandy region was not his vacation spot. Nicknamed "The Red Circle," the 71<sup>st</sup> later liberated Gunskirchen, a subcamp of a concentration camp in Austria. The books and papers he kept revealed photos of living skeletons, piles of bone-thin bodies, and empty eyes laid bare. *N'oublie jamais.*[xxxiv]

Towards the end of 2021, about a year and a half into the global pandemic of COVID-19, many small cabins continue to cluster in the northwest side of Pine Grove to Dogwood Lane, past the Little Red School House and further, to a stand of pines and firs towering above a huge meadow. The expanse of rolling grasses—with its concave back and ninety-degree curve—creates the perfect shape of a baseball field. In the '70s, my friend Joe and I ventured, with wooden bats, baseballs, Budweisers, and Coors, to its clusters of tules, amid flocks of red-winged blackbirds. We pitched, hit, and chased fly balls in the outfield. We likened those days to playing baseball in the 19<sup>th</sup> century. That pastoral field of dreams became the fire's pathway.

I keep hearing the same story about how the 2015 Valley Fire spread so quickly that swirling winds took hold in that dry and treasured bog and fanned flames up the hill to South Hoberg Drive, Hoberg's and other neighborhoods, burning its way past Loch Lomond. The sheer grit of the firefighters saved Loch Lomond and Pine Grove for future generations.

# HOBERG'S
## LAKE COUNTY

This card is from July 10, 1947. The picture was captured by Bud Taylor, a roving photographer, who preserved the family histories of resort guests. Note the server's uniform in the full dining room, tablecloths, and filled glasses of milk. At that time, my mother, Muriel, was a single mother and "the pioneer" in our family for discovering Hoberg's. Muriel is second from the right; her Aunt Flo is on the left with my brother, Jack.

*Photographs of Vacation Moments by C. L. "Bud" Taylor - Also at Seigler Springs*

On our way out the door: the home sky of September 12, 2015.
California is burning (Valley Fire).

# Seven Shades of Green
## Valley Fire

Warm night, light sleep, and early to rise. The dryness of the house, barely cooled from the night before, foreshadows the coming danger. Heat climbs quickly in through the open window. Before diving into our workday—the computer age gives us freedom—we deem the time ripe for a bike ride. Sarah and I set forth to Middletown Trailside Nature Preserve, land of a thousand shade trees, at the corner of Dry Creek Road and Highway 175.

The park, 107 acres of trails, rattlesnake grasses, and shadowed blue sky, spreads through timbers, seven miles down the mountain from Cobb. After a hairpin right on Dry Creek, we slow to 20 in the spotted light. On the way to the parking lot, we sneak under the line of giant oaks that cool our truck in merciful shade, unload the bikes, and head south. Deep into her musical score day and night, like a stone shot from a sling, the ride becomes Sarah's recipe for freedom.

Soon, shadows gather in clusters of shades cast by oaks, pines, black walnut, and a few eye-level manzanita groves that bush out from the park's pathways. Every now and then, a noble madrone cascades near a fleshy painted concrete bench, a rest spot for hikers and horseback riders.

Further through the park, the EcoArts Sculpture Walk reveals many ingenious creations. Far into years of drought and highly aware of climate change, the artists in this sculpture garden have created a myriad of scenes made from organic discards. The likeness of falling rain, its silver strands wandering under clouds tumble in the occasional breeze. It wafts rain-showering streams of sparkling silver light, cooling us off in a transcendent way. We peer through the spaces between the rain channels and see

51

magnified heat waves, undulating in stark contrast to the severe blue sky: oppressive, antagonistic, and cloudless.

A heart made of silk. Large enough to stand in, the jaws of a shark with a heart of pearly silk. Sarah climbs inside the jaws of the heart and spreads her arms as if growing wings. Light-hearted play ricochets off the backdrop of impending disaster. The nudging, scratching, poking concerns of drought, dryness, and vigilance are companions for our bike ride in the park. Three or four hours from now—when the butterflies in our guts transform into passenger pigeons—we'll flee the Valley Fire with blues notes in our mouths and smoke in our throats.

We'll miss these trees that stand as elders, ever so near like a neighboring village of ancestors, whispering at the edge of town, hunched or upright in their familiar paths and corners, waiting for us as friends and family to visit them at any hour.

After a rest, we roll onto our bikes, and Sarah takes off as some invisible force propels her at a furious speed. Her head down, as if pushing past civilization itself, she advances through the dirt-ways, leading by a wide margin, spinning her treadles past the "Rattlesnake Warning" sign, far to the southern perimeter at the edge of the park. From there, the land runs long and deep through hot, dry grasslands and timber, empty seasonal wetlands and vernal pools, past the pole barns and the sheds, the active vineyards, the farms, and the chateau, until it crosses Dry Creek. We corral our breaths, gaze at the beauty and the warning signs, and gather our water cans. On the dirt trail back to the parking lot, we mutter encouragement. Rolling along, riding in the dirt lane, we arrive at the truck, sitting empty among a few cars.

Seven shades of forest green miles later, we are back at the house as another extreme drought malady takes over the day. Bursts of hot wind whoosh out of nowhere; it becomes a perfect day for a fire, right before our eyes. A trail of trees bellows out a language of urgency. The barren maple dropped its dying yellow leaves far too early—in August! More trees speak up in flashes of hot wind. The Red Delicious tree with fruit the size of crabapples hasn't borne healthy fruit in years. Another sacrifice for firewood in the making. The empty maple trembles and slackens its bare limbs; a giant pine rocks enough to hear its bark creak.

Awkward stillness … we see it all, take it all in, and feel sick. A strangeness in this wind. A mass of heat moving at high speed. Shaken by this, the bay tree shifts and bends forward. Quiet. An odd sequence I'd never seen. Some call it evil wind. It suddenly grips a tree that is helpless to run away and shakes it silly.

Drought has been the story for years. The earth of leaves, rock, and pine needles is so dry it crunches as you walk. Everything crackles underfoot. Trees fall limp, downward and sad—the lavender and rosemary, listless. One vacant winter after another follows each long, hot summer. Surely luck has run out and trouble is on the way. Most neighbors are on fire watch; I look for fires around every corner. New rules to live by. No candles or tea lights on deck rails. No open fires. The previous night, I had smelled smoke and circled the property looking for a fire. I thought my neighbor Rick was lighting a barbecue. His wife, Carol, told me later he hadn't been cooking that night.

Today it happens. A pounding—the knock bombs my siesta—on the front door from the veteran Rick. His eyebrows lie as still as iron paint above recoiled lids; and his pupils bore holes through my courtesy.

Black centers stare straight ahead with no hint of movement or cheer. "You see the smoke over there?" he asks. I can't, so I push past the door to the deck: brownish clouds of smoke wailing in from the west of Cobb, thrashing like a muscular monster with ten foreboding arms.

"They're talking about evacuating. And by the looks of this sky, we better start packing." He looks back up at the sinister sight; then, Sarah joins our watch. We stand; horror strikes. "Oh my God, it's blowing right over us!" she exclaims. Smoke is expanding overhead, in confused time lapses, turns, and spirals. Then BaBOOM. Silence. Boom. MEGA BOOM. "Better get your belongings together. Call us if you need anything." He marches back home, no bend in his body.

The enlarged map, while a bit fuzzy, highlights the enormity of the Starview subdivision in 1957. Unfortunately, it and most of the homes were destroyed in the Valley Fire of 2015. Rebuilding continues. The Gifford Springs Road of today was Gifford's Creek Road back then, but some remember it as Gifford's Ranch Road.[xxxv]. (Curiously, in the middle-right rectangle, "Resort" is penciled in.)

At the time of the Kincade Fire, the
Heart on Highway 29 collapsed.

## Bajo Lluvia Musical
### Incendio del Valle

*Ay, mi querida, mi amor*
Nos sentamos junto al fuego—
tú con tu Apple,
yo con deseo.
Eres tú a quien adoro.

*Ay, mi querida, mi amor*
Bajo lluvia musical:
aquí por la noche, se fue mi hambre,
platos vacíos de la comida que preparaste.
Eres tú a quien admiro.

*El camino correcto cambia cada vuelta,*
*el lugar que pensamos perdido es el lugar a donde volvimos,*
*como el diamante que nos entregó un extraño en camino,*
*al fin nuestro hogar fuera de peligro del incendio.*

*Ay, mi querida, mi amor*
Te despiertas de una deriva,
boca seca, labios resecos;
te traigo guayaba y miel.
Soy yo a quien inspiras.

*Ay, mi querida, mi amor*
Te vas a dormir,
sed abierto del beso de néctar.
Barcos de vela y relámpagos esperan tus sueños.

# Under Musical Rain
## Valley Fire

*Oh, mi querida, mi amor*
We sit by the fire—
you with your Apple,
me with desire.
It is you I adore.

*Oh, mi querida, mi amor*
Under musical rain:
in for the night, out of hunger,
plates empty of the food you made.
It is you I admire.

*The high road changes every turn,*
*the place we thought lost is the place where we returned,*
*like the diamond handed us by a roadside stranger,*
*our home at last out of fire's danger.*

*Oh, mi querida, mi amor*
You awaken from a drift,
mouth dry, parched lips;
I bring you guava and honey.
It is I you inspire.

*Oh, mi querida, mi amor*
You wander off to sleep,
thirst wet from the kiss of nectar.
Sailing ships and lightning bolts await your dreams.

# Return to the Eye of the Storm
## Valley Fire

Our mood grew somber as we numbed out at the destruction on the first drive back to Cobb after a 13-day forced evacuation. A few hundred feet beyond Dry Creek, on the cutoff, the road narrowed to one lane and was lined with heavy dump trucks. The machines stood out like a train of gladiators, resting overnight before battle. An impossible task, loading the ruins of the Valley Fire and hauling them somewhere else.

Slow going on Dry Creek Road to Highway 175: past tires the size of hefty boulders, tractors looking two stories tall, chrome pipes reaching for the stars. A road of giants toting buckets the size of bone-dry creek beds. Those trucks were a rare galactic army on many wheels, a fearless and muscular presence sent to rescue what lay burned beyond grotesque.

Our major concerns were the High Road cabin, Hardester's, Forest Lake, Carol and Rick's, names and places from the old neighborhood: Johnson, Keys, Halligan, O'Conner, Axelrod, Cain, Bev and Ed, Hoberg's, Starview, Pine Grove—the whole mountain for that matter.

We motored up the steep incline of High Road to the original family cabin, shock absorbers intact. The '60s western chalet, built by Curly Webb in 1962, was sold in '82 to my friend Steven Axelrod, with whom I owned a small percentage for five years. Curly built another western chalet home on lower High Road and a few others around Cobb. In the enduring ones, large, angled windows run under the vaulted roofline above perimeter walls to allow its residents and guests to gaze at forest views in sun and shaded light. That Circle of Life Loop—High Road to Schwartz Road, with its companions of evergreen trees and cabins, fortunes of ladybugs heaped in piles to keep warm, twin year-round creeks, and moss-covered stones— thrives, unbroken.

The firefighters lit a backfire on the Cobb Water property across the road from the High Road cabin and saved the neighborhood a lot of grief. We circled back down the shaded hill; moss stones and pine needles turned the dark ground rusty. Farther down High Road, the past and present merged before me. I searched for the horse corral, where the trail herd leaned and dozed in different directions, an innate behavior for prey animals. Ground squirrels claimed the land after the horses were led to abandon the flat ground of today's Village Inn.

A woman interviewed on live news the night of the fire reported the gas station had blown up and Hardester's Market burned to the ground. Desperately, I headed there to see for myself. On the way over, I ruminated about its history when the store was first built. It began with someone's plan to develop a bigger market than the "little store" once housed in the shell of the Village Pub. Decades ago, while the foundation was underway, constructed and formed with wood stakes, streamers, mudsill, and the mighty Douglas fir, a splendid store rose on the graded plateau. Once completed, the spacious new market drew us through its doors. Cobb residents welcomed it with open arms. My dad was among the first. I remembered how he raved about the new store. He'd call me. "You've got to see this," he'd say. It was his dream to shop there—his Cobb Mountain dream had become the reality now known to everyone as Hardester's.

When Sarah and I arrived in the parking lot, I leapt from the truck and through Hardester's doors to witness the clerks and customers and search the produce, aisles, coolers, and stocked shelves—for what, I did not know. The outpost spoke its true character on the way in: a statement at the entrance declared they would not be abandoning ship. Not burned to the ground. Still here. Period.

Cobb Village and a few other locales survived; most homes in the neighborhood above Black Rock Golf Course made it. Three roads up and so many other neighborhoods did not fare as well. We took a drive past the surviving school, through the deep black forest to the corner of Summit and Hoberg Drive South, where my family had lived after selling their original cabin.

A roadblock greeted us; through the haze we felt in body and spirit, we told our tale and were waved through. At first, I wasn't sure I found the right house on Summit Drive. The topography looked like France in the World War II books my father kept till the day he died. The air, weighed down in its own toxicity, was quiet, heavy, suffocating, and rancid—masks mandatory. This scene of utter bleakness pushed us into despair and into an unknown level of futility. The home I helped my father move into and maintain was distorted into ashes, concrete, and infinite nothingness.

When I arrived at the South Hoberg property, my eyes denied where I was, but my legs remembered the hike up the driveway; I knew I had the right house. No entryway nor balcony existed. The only remains were the steel pole of a mournful basketball hoop; the melted plastic backboard resembled a dripping phantom's face. This sight would have devastated my parents, as this home held beloved memories.

One such recollection took place in the kitchen and dining room where our blended-five family prepared and shared our last meal, a day or two before Thanksgiving in 1988. In the years after Mother Muriel passed into night's waiting arms, I gathered in the kitchen with my father or my son Casey and his friends; other times, I went alone with a notebook or a guitar to keep an eye on things when my father was out of town. Imagine arriving at a family home you barely recognize! Landmarks—vanished and

61

non-existent—like everything else, they were mangled beyond recognition. The entirety of Cobb knows the scene. Residents of any place and all places, counties, and towns trampled by dragons know the scene. We fight the battle. Climate change.

Up the street sprawled the artistically designed home of our once neighbors and life-long friends, Bev and Ed. Before moving back to what proved to be their surviving log cabin near the school, Ed and Bev built a spectacular place on South Hoberg with a panoramic view of the valley. The fire had climbed the hill and wolfed it down along with most of the region. The war veterans would call that "wiped out."

In the middle of the twisted metal, burnt, disfigured trees, and concrete rubble, one house survived. An American flag slacked outside. A dog barked inside. All the other homes, lots, and their landscapes were shattered, unidentifiable.

We had to drive to Hoberg's Resort, where my mother Muriel, single woman with two boys in tow, first stayed in the 1940s. We crossed over Emerford Road to reach it, walked up to the fence that surrounded the entire catastrophe, and stared blankly. Like all the other areas we observed that day, quiet nothingness looked back at us from this obliterated place of joy. The land that people booked a year ahead. This once celebrated resort that thrived far beyond the imagination of excellence, class, and innovation.

How many families visit a place in a hundred years? At least thousands went to Hoberg's, slept in the cabins, ate in the cafés and restaurants. Tommy Dorsey played there. And Harry James. Sal Carson brought his summertime orchestra to perform at the Pine Bowl, a bandstand under the stars. Luther Burbank walked the summer grounds. Visitors flew in from all places. Driving from Hoberg's past Loch Lomond and Seigler's led to the lingering open field of the once thriving Paul Hoberg Airport.[xxxvi]

The Hoberg's sign lasted through the firestorm the way the figure on the road at Starview had stood through it all. These symbols endured more real hell than myth could invent, with complete mockery of the origins that began in the hearts and minds of their creators.

At the far side of Hoberg's resort grounds, a foot or so above ground level, the blue stripe of the pool's side remained intact; everything else was at the bitter end and out of proportion to common sense. A clean-up took months to begin and years to clear. Hoberg's got the worst of things. Staring at the road again, we headed back home; we'd had enough. The next day, we didn't visit Anderson Springs. That would have been morbid curiosity without purpose. We weren't sightseeing; we were finding our roots in the piles of ashes we visited. We would go to Loch Lomond and Pine Grove later in natural time and see multi-colored "Thank You Firefighters" signs on surviving trees.

After Hoberg's, at a later time I cannot pinpoint, I drove over to Starview, got out of my truck, and looked around. All I saw was the figure in the fountain; the rest of the place was bombed out like Hoberg's. Starview was the last stop of my father, Bob Williams, before he got too timeworn for Cobb life and moved back to Sonoma County. A few minutes later, Barbara drove up. She had known my father for many years. He had frequented Starview on summer afternoons, always leaving before dark. I threw a party for his 80th birthday at Starview for him and his friends, Sarah and I adding our tributes with poetry and music.

Two years later, he was gone from this special piece of earth. Van, Rick, my son Casey, and I scattered half of Bob's ashes at Starview. Rick poured tall, iced drinks at an outdoor table, and we told our stories. "He was a two-drink-a-day man in those days. You knew what time it was when Bob walked through the door," they said. In the shock and destruction, there was little Barbara and I could say. Cobb's convivial face had grown dimly ashen. Tired and heavy black sacks drooped from its fractured, dilated eyes. Starview's marvel of blue picture windows had dissolved into blue marbles sunken in pits of ash. The famously clean Cobb air was so dense and toxic we exchanged our quiet farewells. Barbara stood in the parking lot in total desolation, the ashes of one more storied lodge her sole companion. Nothing held a breath of life for Barbara.

I couldn't drive the road down the hill to the golf course; it was even more grotesque with concrete blocks and incinerated houses and cars. I crept back down to Gifford Springs, grateful that at least Whispering Pines and Forest Lake had survived. By the looks of things, grief had taken over Cobb and post-traumatic stress soon followed.

Hardester's was a place folks ended up after the 13-day wait that began the day after the fire started. Locals picked up coffee and baking soda to clean their refrigerators of rotten food. With what little hope they had, they consoled one another. If not with words, then by a glance, nod, or determined look. A few spoke in whispers and conciliatory hugs at the front of the store. My own shock couldn't hide behind blank, darting eyes.

The elephant in the store had melted, and everyone was feeling it. Any bright thought from a cashier or patron became the holy grail; it was that dark and hopeless outside. Without a statewide effort led by Cal Fire and the water, planes, and red dust, nothing would have survived. Life would have become like *The Road* by Cormac McCarthy.

Too many dreams ended on September 12, 2015, and on the days and nights that followed. It took only the moment I opened my truck door to flee the Valley Fire to appreciate who and what did survive on the legendary, majestic, and hardy landscape of Cobb Mountain, California.

Van, Starview's owner, talks to friends in the bar. He passed
away before the Valley Fire and was spared the tragedy of its loss.

Blue windows, trim, and shingles heighten the theme Van created
from Starview's very name. Poetry Band, the duo of Timothy Williams
and Kevin Haapala, play the song "Cobb Mountain" on the Fourth of
July.

# Déjà Vu... the Night Version
## Tubbs Fire

October 9, 2017. Midnight in Santa Rosa. Working on a critical deadline due in six days. Holly leaves scratch glass, too much scraping and scuffling outside. Branches scramble in the whipping sounds that slap the house windows. A fleeting mob stampedes across the roof, more urgent than the murder of crows that gathers on cold winter days. Grabbing the phone, I text Sarah at Cobb. "I hope our little place is still here tomorrow. There's quite a storm swirling outside." No answer. Text my son. No answer.

Smoke! Where is it coming from? I grab the front door and brace it open with my body. The awe of seeing red everywhere. Eyes peeling back the layers of shock. Choking on toxins. Pull the door shut. The red, far enough away … No need to pack, no need to flee. It's close enough, though. Too close. It's going to be a long one … Fire. Oh no. I remember fire. Déjà vu … the night version.

Familiar? This is different from the Valley Fire. That was percussion, interval, and another mega boom seconds later. Here, it's rumbling across Brush Creek Road, a progression of rolling booms, muffled by space like a fireworks finale that never ends. Successions of shock waves. An overload of bass, standing in the first three rows of a concert by The Who. Baboom, boom. Keith Moon whaling 10 feet away.

Lights blink, blink, drop. Light the tea lights. The gas stove works; the burners bring routine blue flames. Midnight tea. Black and strong. Spoon a double dose of China Keemun. Line up a few belongings near the back door. Wait. Sirens. Sirens. Sirens.

I wander out wearing the bandit's bandana. Highway 12 is packed with cars backed up at the blank, hollow eyes of the traffic light. Monday morning commuters in the middle of the night. It's past closing time at the downtown bars.

The lines of cars keep the rhythm going. One car, then another in four-four time. The accent on the one. One car climbs the sidewalk, tearing past the delicate order. Maybe his wife is in labor.

# Morning Dream Duet
## Tubbs Fire

In the days and nights of the October 2017 Tubbs Fire, Sarah and I worked in two different counties. She was on a songwriting retreat in Lake County, where we both were when the Valley Fire started two years earlier, and I was in my office working on a major deadline in Sonoma County. She saw deep-blue Lake County sky and had full electric and phone. In Sonoma County, spreading across many counties, the Tubbs and other fires were raging out of control. I paced as menacing winds tossed swirling branches on my roof and felt many shock waves from Fountain Grove blowing up. Wild red flames climbed the sky as I breathed the relentless smoke and northern Santa Rosa burned. With no electricity for three days and nights, I lived by candlelight, waking to the taste of wet ashes—minor irritations compared to what so many people continue to go through to this very day. Sarah and I called each other over the backyard fences of our neighboring counties. Smoke jammed our cell phones and our calls dropped as certain as stones. We texted the musings of a poem, and in the chasm of conflicting realities, a duet came to light:

**TW**  *Mi cielo*, I'm right beside you. The fire has burned for days, the setting sun has turned red, and smoke has imperiled our breath. Do you feel the warm waft in the room? Do you feel my breath near your ear, my passion?

**SB**  Yes, I feel you, darling. Warm.

**TW**  Do you feel my arm around your waist, my sweating hand in yours, as we walk to the window, *mi amor*?

**SB**  Yes, my love, I see the window.

**TW**  Will you sing for me? Your voice carries water to my scorched heart. Your voice makes me feel like a high-flying dove in the rain.

**SB**  I will sing my new song for you.

**TW**  I love your singing, and your songs bring me home. They make me feel that in a single day anything can turn and we'll stop the firestorm that is trying to devour our county.

**SB**  You are a diamond, but you're not rough. Elevated, generous, I can't get enough. Educated, sophisticated, but you can boogie too! That's why I write 13 bars for you.

**TW**  The night sky slept dark, a long way from calm, till the copper-lit dawn knocked at the moment we untangled our dreams. I left for the window to meet you in the morning haze.

**SB**  Smoke and fire have stolen our days, neighborhoods, country roads, horses, pets, and our lives.

**TW**  Morning light weeps from your smoky-blue eyes, my love, for tomorrow's clouds to shape into rain.

# Sombras de Velas Encendidas
## El Incendio de Tubbs

Sombras de velas encendidas
pasando la barra de la cocina
en los rincones de la habitación.
Escritas sobre las paredes
con manos ardientes,
letras deterioradas por el tiempo
y finales tristes.

Corrige las reglas de la Tierra.
Repara el daño del La Tierra.
Ama
a la Madre Tierra
como nunca.

Ella sobrevive,
está cicatrizada;
sus vestimentas están desgastadas.

Vidas desgarradas.

Su rostro lleva
las fisuras del tiempo
en el gran siglo actual
de humo e incendios.

Uno puede repelar
la furia implacable del fuego
y frustrar su camino destrozado
hasta que vuelva al suelo salvaje de la Tierra

cuando vertemos el agua encima
y vertemos el agua encima…

hasta que se nos agote el agua.

**Candles in a mirror increased available light during the blackout.**

## Candlelight Shadows
### Tubbs Fire

Candlelit shadows
past the kitchen counter
in the room's corners.
Written upon walls
with fiery hands,
time-worn letters
and sad endings.

Mend Earth's rules.
Repair Earth's damage.
Love
Mother Earth
like never before.

She survives,
is scarred;
her garments are worn.

Lifetimes torn.

Her face bears
the fissures of time
in the grand present century
of smoke and fires.

One can beat back
the fire's relentless fury
and thwart its mangled path
back into earth's savage ground

when we pour the water on
and pour the water on…

until we run out of water.

73

# Night of Poetry and Song
## Tubbs Fire

As we emerged from the gloom of the Tubbs fire knowing many residents who lost everything, I got a call from artist Penelope La Montagne.[xxxvii] Penelope and Cynthia Helen Beecher were putting together an event featuring poets and musicians called, A Firestorm of Words ("an evening of Healing & High-Heart"). She asked for a song or poem to contribute to an evening at Healdsburg Center for the Arts on Plaza Street in Healdsburg, Friday, December 1, 2017.

Penelope and Cynthia called on artists who strode quietly to the mic. The tribute ran long into the night. Our purpose was to address the catastrophe we hoped would never return yet knew was still at our backs. Jack Burton sang a new song. Poems and songs gave gallery drop-ins room to wander around the paintings and sculptures while listening.

Students from West Side and Alexander Valley Elementary Schools read poems. One boy, talented beyond his years, ran his elegant hands across the fretboard; his melodic guitar softened the grieving house as he revealed with each note a brief escape from our collective sorrow. Karl Frederick's poem took us on his escape from Coffey Park to the freeway. An uncertain feeling swept over him, evident as his shoulders pulled in and his body sagged while he read. On the night of the fire, he had no idea where he was going. Jackie Huss, who writes and teaches in Sonoma County, talked about her midnight in October, racing the flames while loading her aging mother into the car.

A prior composing commitment kept Sarah from attending. With her blessing, Penelope La Montagne read Sarah's part in my poem, "Morning Dream Duet." We stood side by side, Penelope's Buddha soul present. She spoke with poem in hand, her long golden-rose hair falling freely to her shoulders and kind ocean eyes peering into the moment. Wonderful Penelope, who gave so much to other artists, always with a higher purpose in mind, passed away a few short months later in 2018. She shared her own poems, and the air above our seats filled with that sound—the quiet hum of music playing in the intervals, the sound of minds listening. Quiet music till the finish, past the endings, shedding the armors and masks of our collective vigilance. Cynthia read a poem of loss and renewal from her book, *Send Me No Ants*.

> "Winter's calling
> lie down at my roots
> nurture spring shoots."[xxxviii]

We filtered back to our suffering towns, having broken through to the other side, grateful after walking the coals, relieved until morning from the daily dread, and waking with the reek and the taste of damp ashes.

Compelled by the night of poetry and song, I called more and more friends to check in. They had plenty to say. I heard back from my friend, Bernadette, an Oakmont resident, who—with her elderly dog and a neighbor—evacuated to a gas station parking lot. After a day there, the fire department knocked on their car window and ordered them to evacuate again. Three different "safe" homes took them in, and three different times they heard the pounding on the door and had to flee. After 14 days and 13 nights, they, too, returned home.

Rod Hagge, a longtime friend and trusted farrier, told me the saga of Cloverleaf Ranch: "They saved the horses while the house burned down."

I called friends near Mark West Springs Road who live in a villa embellished by their own handmade painted tile. As if belonging in a 19th century setting, the villa rises on a narrow road that crosses a creek; the fire department saved their landscape and home.

My friend Lars, who also lived off Mark West Springs Road, lost everything. During the fire, he left his house on his motorcycle to survey the surrounding neighborhood. Detained at a barricade by the fire department, he was forbidden to return. His house burned to the ground along with his baseball history, heirlooms, artwork, and musical instruments.

Upper Parker Hill Road and Fountaingrove Parkway became a ghost drive through a graveyard: hardly a breath of life as I passed the tombstones of this neighborhood's dream of vistas and open spaces.

A friend in Coffey Park told me about walls of flames spreading house to house. Winds tossed fire balls and chased him through the voids of the streets as he evacuated the neighborhood. His home survived. Decimated childhood treasures and vast collections, recovered cats and dogs, downed organic farms and rescued sheep, and the many stories not yet told reverberated daily throughout the town.

Two years later, when a friend showed me her new kitchen cabinet designs and floor plans, the future looked brighter. Another guy sold the lot where his house was demolished; he'd had enough of wildfires and moved on. One couple gathered uncovered remaining valuables, still uncertain and confused about their next steps. Shortly after, I heard from our friend, Kristine Sudduth, who—in less than two years after losing home and history—said, "This summer, cooler than last, has been everything I love about Sonoma County."

Then on October 23, 2019, it hit again. The Kincade Fire burst forth. Smoke once again at night. Among other things, it nearly took out the town of Windsor. During that spell of high winds and PG&E preventative blackouts, panic rang out in Cobb when an early morning fire started on Rainbow Lane in Pine Grove. It became another desperate hour.[xxxix] Lucky for us, the Cobb Fire Department was on the scene in minutes and smothered the house fire before it left the property. A fire, in pre-dawn wind howling around Cobb, would spell disaster for the mountain's own survival.

Sonoma County took the brunt of the Kincade smoke—the blaze hit their side of the mountain. Both sides of the Mayacamas Mountains sustained heavy losses.

> "And one by one the nights
> between our separated cities are
> joined into the night that unites us."[xl]

The Kincade Fire and, in 2021, the Dixie Fire brought smoke that clung to trees, vanished by night, and seeped under windows before dawn. We live near meadow or mountain, watch for fires, and listen to wind shifts in our sleep. Earth burning. Australia burning. The Amazon burning. California burning.

## La Noche Calmada
### El Incendio de Tubbs

Cuando te deslizas en medio de nosotros desde el Pacífico,
el mundo se calma;
ciudades y pueblos saborean tu azul profundo.

Cuando tu neblina se ilumina,
estrellas con vestidos de noche al crepúsculo
se atenúan sobre nuestras colinas retorcidas y ennegrecidas.
Árboles temblorosos y desnudos se desvanecen;
farolas encendidas como las colas de cometas se derriten.

*Y respiras más noche, impulsando la noche de viento-costero,*
*quitando de nuestras mentes caóticas los recuerdos.*

Caminamos, corrimos o condujimos lejos de las calles envueltas en llamas
a las carreteras pavimentadas, todo el humo despreciable y las noticias
impactantes más siniestras que nuestras huidas. Escapamos hacia lo
desconocido, y hemos recorrido esas rutas desde entonces,
hasta aprender una y otra vez la secuela.
Olvidada ya en la vasta y lenta neblina.

*Y respiras más noche, impulsando la noche de viento-costero,*
*quitando de nuestras mentes caóticas los recuerdos.*

Fantasmas silenciosos aparecen, bordes cubiertos en carmesí,
borrando carteleras de horror, dragones, y obsesiones.

Mañana al mediodía, las cortinas se levantarán.
Regresarán las colinas abandonadas y los árboles huecos,
dañados y heridos y en caos turbulento.
Vueltos de los incendios y las batallas libradas
a toda velocidad contra ellos.

*Y respiras más noche, impulsando la noche de viento-costero,*
*quitando de nuestras mentes caóticas los recuerdos.*

# Quieting Night
## Tubbs Fire

When you glide in among us from the Pacific,
the world settles down;
cities and towns relish your deepening blue.

When your fog glows in,
stars in dusk's evening gowns
dim over our twisted, blackened hills.
Shivering naked trees vanish;
streetlights lit like comets' tails melt away.

*And you breathe more night and further the coast-wind night,*
*pushing from our shambolic minds the memories.*

We walked, ran, or drove from the fire-blown streets to the paved
highways, all the wretched smoke and shocking news
more ominous than our flights. We escaped to the unknown,
and have rerun those routes ever since,
until we learned again and again the fallout.
Forgotten now in the vast, slow fog.

*And you breathe more night and further the coast-wind night,*
*pushing from our shambolic minds the memories.*

Silent phantoms wander in, edges draped in scarlet,
erasing billboards of horror, dragons, and obsessions.

Around noon tomorrow, the curtains will lift.
The abandoned hills and hollow trees will come back,
injured and wounded and in turbulent chaos.
Back from the fires and the full-throttle battles
waged against them.

*And you breathe more night and further the coast-wind night,*
*pushing from our shambolic minds the memories.*

SUNDAY, DECEMBER 2ND 1-7PM

# OUT OF THE FIRE

**SARAH BAKER**      **DOUG JAYNE**
**LEVI LLOYD**      **WILLY JORDAN**
**VOLKER STRIFLER**      **EKI SHOLA**
**DANNY SORENTINO**      **THE ABOLITIONISTS**
**JOHNNY CAMPBELL**      **ALLEGRA BROUGHTON**

LIVE MUSIC ~ RAFFLE ~ SILENT AUCTION

**PROCEEDS BENEFIT THE**
**OUT OF THE FIRE TRUST FUND**
FOR THE REPLACEMENT OR REPAIR OF
MUSICAL INSTRUMENTS
LOST OR DAMAGED IN THE NORTH BAY WILDFIRES

**$10 adv GA/ $25 VIP Dinner & Show ($15/$30 Door)**

**Tix at OutOfTheFire2018.Eventbrite.com**

 1100 Valley House Dr
Rohnert Park (707) 665-9472

Publicity photo for the Out of the Fire Benefit.
Left to right: Johnny Campbell, Volker Strifler, Gary Silva,
Allegra Broughton, Sam Page, Sarah Baker, Glen Sullivan, Rick
Clifford, Levi Lloyd, and Doug Jayne. Not pictured: Danny Sorentino,
Willy Jordan, Eki Shola, Mooka Rennick and The Abolitionists, and
Zero. (Photo by Kathleen McCallum.)

Opposite page:
Event poster by Artist, Stanley Mouse. Graphics by Casey Williams.

# Out of the Fire
## Tubbs Fire

After the 2017 Tubbs Fire, Mark "Mooka" Rennick, owner of a Sonoma landmark, Prairie Sun Recording Studios, called a plethora of musicians, most of them from Sonoma County. His vision was to record an album of new songs, eventually named *Out of the Fire* after the title track by my wife, Sarah Baker. Mark Rennick, Allen Sudduth, and Sarah coproduced the album at Mooka's studios. As another shining example of musicians and the music community uniting for a cause, these gatherings have become a tradition in the artistically bountiful Sonoma County, California. Proceeds from sales of the album funded the distribution of instruments, resources, and money into the hands of musicians and teachers of music who lost pianos, horns, guitars, and recording equipment.

Sarah Baker, Volker Strifler, Levi Lloyd, Danny Sorentino, Johnny Campbell, Doug Jayne, Willy Jordan, Eki Shola, Solid Air, and Zero all offered songs for *Out of the Fire*. When the recording was completed and packaged, they held two benefit fundraisers. The first was held at Prairie Sun Recording, with outdoor performance stages and open spaces, located in southwest Cotati near the Petaluma border. Hidden within a backdrop of cool summer weather, Prairie Sun owes its existence to Mooka. Its elements include first-growth redwood barns and chicken coops that have flourished across the rolling Sonoma County countryside since the last century. That day, country cottages, oak trees, lawn, flower gardens, and the extraordinary history of recorded music, coalesced into the famed destination. Tom Waits has a studio named after him at Prairie Sun, one of his recording haunts, and many other prominent clients contribute to its considerable standing in the music world.

Musical instruments and the musicians that played them traveled the path of the benefit's cause, a swath of hope in the burned-up Sonoma County landscape. The lesser, dearer things that were saved, precious things that fit into one's hand, became symbols of survival. The vibe of the event was like "A Place Called Home," the Doug Jayne and Allen Sudduth song[xli] by the same name. The gathering itself was a testament to the relief a positive event can bring after a tragic one. In "Best Things," Johnny Campbell sang that "the best things in life ain't things at all," and Solid Air soared to new heights singing "Home," by Karla Bonoff. Eminent artist Stanley Mouse, who designed the artwork for the album, listened to the music and signed a few CDs. The Marin County band, Zero, which has roots back to 1980—and 50 people dancing at the foot of the stage—closed the show.

Sally Tomatoes, the comedy club, restaurant, and event destination, held the second benefit. "Sally's," located south of Sonoma State University on the old Hewlett Packard campus, is owned by entrepreneurs Gerard Giudice, who was elected Mayor of Rohnert Park, California in 2020, and businessman, Bill Pettibone. Katrina Markarian, Nancy Pritchard, and Sarah Baker worked tirelessly to put together this second show, using most of the same production crew and musicians as the first.

It was an optimal space for the event: the spacious room, stage, and loose seating lent easy access to food and drink. Outside on wide paths, patrons had room to walk around the patios and lawns. Beneath its corporate exterior, Sally Tomatoes offered what is cherished in Sonoma and Lake Counties—its own character and plenty of room to wander.

It provided ideal ingredients for a group motivated to contribute to the cause, as well as the space to stray and discover the potential of renewal. Healing a community in the aftermath of the fire.

Sarah played at both shows and, though Willy Jordan couldn't make it, Levi Lloyd, Volker Strifler, Gary Silva, Eki Shola, and most of the players on the record from the first show played. A surprise guest attended after playing a round of golf downtown: the gracious Harold Jones, Tony Bennett and Count Basie's drummer, sat in with the band.

Casey Williams, who had performed and hosted many comedy performances at Sally Tomatoes, emceed. I read the firefighter poem from this collection at both events. Kristine Sudduth recited her poem, too. About the Tubbs fire, it begins:

> *I saw a lot of sadness yesterday*
> My burned down house
> People needing food and caring
> A man dying alone[xlii]

Poetry had joined forces with music, always a medicinal confluence. Sonoma County rose out of the ashes like its northern neighbor, Lake County, proving that the two counties share the peril of wildfires and the aftermaths of healing.

# Turning Forward Once Again

After the Valley and Tubbs Fires, the Kincade Fire sent everybody packing all over again as about 190,000 of us were evacuated. Then came the Glass Fire Complex just before COVID-19 made us all stay home. Finally, the Dixie Fire cemented the permanence of smoke in the atmosphere. We lived it morning, noon—and at night, the stars disappeared for weeks on end.

Fortunately, after the Valley Fire, the people of Cobb had begun using the practices of "Defensible Space" (an area maintained to reduce fire damage), such as following a path of personal and civic regulation, clearing brush to 100 feet around property, and trimming trees above the roof, which are small pieces of the challenge to survival. Prevention. Attention. Dedication. In Firewise[xliii] neighborhoods, reinforcement of those principles flows abundantly, and *Firewise.org* provides practices for protecting the landscape. In addition, new homes and neighborhoods are framed with new building codes. One finds familiar landmarks—Cobb Village and Loch Lomond—standing tall.

The Valley Fires's surviving historical resorts persevere by the grace of a shift of wind, and by the brave efforts of neighbors, volunteers, inmate crews, and Cal Fire: Whispering Pines, Pine Grove, Loch Lomond, Seigler Springs, and others. The Hoberg's property, however, became a home for hundreds of downed trees, and truckloads of the burned-up trees were given to survivors for firewood. In a year's time, hummingbirds, ravens, and deer returned. Forest Lake Resort also remains closed to the public, and the water flowing from its premises continues to be a coveted commodity, being sold and resold over the last six years.

As climate change causes the fires to start earlier, end later, and burn more intensely and extensively, residents insist on timely updates about their favorite businesses and staying apprised of fire danger or bears in the neighborhood. Facebook groups such as *Cobb Mountain Rising, Cobb Friends and Family, Friends of Cobb Mountain, Visit Kelseyville,* and *Cobb Mountain Area Historical Society* are daily resources and communication centers, catering to those who wish to reminisce about the romantic era of the resorts' golden years, post photos of shared childhood memories, celebrate the rebuilding of businesses, protect Cobb's natural areas, and support recreational activities, among other things. More Facebook groups are sprouting up all the time.

In an effort to preserve the area's history, a longtime resident of Cobb, Peter M.J. Hess, PhD, is editing memoirs of a collectively-authored volume entitled *Cobb Valley School,* about the Little Red Schoolhouse or simply, "Little Red." He is working on three projects simultaneously; the second is a pictorial history of Cobb for the Images of America book series. His third is a multi-authored work entitled *Cobb Mountain Region: A Social History.* It will live primarily online at the *Cobb Mountain Area Historical Society* Facebook page that he cofounded with firefighter Richie Bucher.

Demonstrating Cobb Mountain's spirit—with the backing of loyal locals—some surviving resorts have reopened. Reclaimed as a cabin retreat, Pine Grove was so packed on Labor Day 2020 that patrons had to park further away and walk. A few resorts are booking reservations, and several years after the Valley Fire, it's still a good place to purchase a lot and build a home or buy an existing one among creeks and stones.

On some days, the clear, cool creek breeze wells up, and the hands on the clock that turned backward turn forward once again. Springs all over Cobb Mountain, natural resources from Cobb Mountain's soul, sing the same sounds the resorts once heard. And they are no less golden to an ear that hears its sweet music in the night breezes, mixed with occasional howling wolves.

Those voices in the wind, by oral tradition, pass the stories of romance, spring water, and resorts along the way. Like Jennifer, a Hardester's staff member, said after the evacuation was lifted, "Everybody at Cobb has a story to tell." Similarly, Gaye LeBaron, of Santa Rosa's the *Press Democrat*, wrote that people need to talk about the fires. I decided to follow that wisdom and asked every person I knew about their experiences, and their stories poured forth. The details in this book are but one forged memory in a boundless mosaic. And just like Forest Lake's

 Spring Water, may the energy, hope, and passion of our community keep surging forth and turning forward.

# Epilogue: Secret Waters

On a cool spring afternoon, Jim Steinke—in an olive green fedora, cotton plaid shirt, long saddle-fawn coat, and rusty corduroy slacks—walks around the neighborhood picking a 1921 Gibson mandolin with a fleur-de-lis inlaid between its eight keys. Last winter, he celebrated the first year in his new home after his old place in Anderson Springs burned to the ground in the Valley Fire.

Before the foot of winter snow fell, earlier in the summer—wearing slacks and a white shirt with black piping—he introduced himself, his guitar, and amp to the neighborhood by playing Bach, Mozart, and his teacher Jorma Kaukonen's "Embryonic Journey" from his deck. In the night air, the richness of his strings stands out from the distant gush of Jones Creek. As he saunters up the road, he calls for the few kept cats he knows, and his eyes search for them, especially the one whose name tag reads "Little"—a cream-and-nutmeg-patched, seventeen-year-old matriarch of the mountain. "Have you seen Little?" he asks.

The past and future emerge in voices from the homes along Jim's trek. An ambitious girl named Lila rides by on her blue bicycle. In lyrical tones—her voice tuned by the Tibetan singing bowls in her home—she answers, "We haven't seen her!" She pedals on, an allegro con spirito follows. Her mother, strolling behind, announces, "Adam's Springs has finished rebuilding and it's beautiful!" Another neighbor strides up and declares, "Little's out hunting dandelions," adding that the Summit Pool is open for swimming. A third person exclaims, "Little will persevere, but I hear a bear was seen heading for Robert's house!" Neighborhood voices filter through Jim's mandolin, and his music lightens the woes of the world. Jim's fingers pick the strings and we listen as the springs ramble and flow underfoot.

A guy opens his front door and says, "You know, Pine Grove's cold pool was built in the '20s. Imagine. A hundred years!" From her plumeria-red-anteroom library, a well traveled writer offers this vision: "Black Rock [the oldest golf course in Lake County] will sell to the State Parks. They'll hire local folks to create a destination oasis of gardens, showgrounds, and trails."

A next-door neighbor wistfully tells Jim that he longs for a Forest Lake Resort comeback. "Yes, but have you seen the parking lot at Mandala Springs, a wellness retreat center in Cobb? It's jam-packed and draws visitors from the same counties as the resorts once welcomed through their doors!" That is the future of Cobb Mountain: businesses have adapted and converted into destinations that facilitate "the interconnectedness of nature and spirit.[xliv]"

Little sits on the high deck,
paws folded under—
a gazing Sphinx.
Her ears shift; she attunes
to every stirring, falling leaf, and living creature.

Some say, "The best kept secret in Lake County is its water."
Calso Water, Shasta, Forest Lake, Cobb Mountain, and Calistoga
Water were some of the brands associated with Forest Lake
Resort. Imagine a sparkling lime and cherry-flavored drink
made from Cobb spring water!

**Great Uncle Jack:**
"Find a rock in a cold creek, crack open a beer,
and put your feet in the water."

**Michele's photo of the view from her tent after evacuating the Kincade Fire. She found a refuge for her and her dogs, safely tucked away from advancing fires.**

# *Coda*
## *by Michele Anna Jordan*

Midnight, late October, 2019. Curled up in a sleeping bag inside a tent. Wind roaring like a freight train. Inside, Lark and Bobby bark themselves hoarse. Outside, wild creatures paw the canvas.

This is the second night of a mandatory evacuation for nearly 200,000 Sonomans, as the Kincade Fire threatens to jump 101 and roar to the coast. I have landed at this 85-acre working farm in southwest Sebastopol, with its fields of indigo and blueberries, its bleating sheep and happy chickens, its mama otter happily munching on crawfish from the creek that intersects the farm, after inching along for over an hour on a drive that takes 10 minutes. A radio announcer says evacuation centers, motels, and hotels are full. Just drive south, police officers urge; San Francisco, fewer than 50 miles south, is now nearly eight hours away. When an impatient driver nearly crashes into me, I swerve into the farm's driveway. A friend rushes to the car, helps me step out, wraps me in blankets, and brings me a warm drink. We sit on the porch of their cookhouse, watching the sun rise, slipping inside when flashing lights approach. We are breaking the law by not leaving the county, but we are safe, well south of any possible fire line, with water hoses that shoot higher than 100 feet.

A native like Timothy, I understand that to be here is to live amidst droughts, floods, and fires. But their pace has quickened, and California's natural cycles are more dire now than they were when we were growing up. As our numbers have grown, we have begun building in canyons, on hillsides, and on mountain tops long avoided because what has happened in the last few years, the fires and their aftermath, has occurred for millennia; it is the nature of our geography. Indigenous peoples, who cared for this land for thousands of years before Europeans arrived, understood that parts of this glorious place were, over the long haul, uninhabitable. Yet we are already rebuilding atop the earth's blackened scars. Will we ever learn?

*Figure on the Road* captures something essential about this quickening, about the impact of climate change on how we live now, about the losses we will continue to suffer. But it is about more than that, too.

Timothy releases the ache at the intersection of loss and memory and, in doing so, accomplishes what all artists struggle to achieve: To transform personal experience into universal connection. Memories glow like a jar of fireflies, escaping, one by one: Long still ghosts rise. Men swap WWII stories, vintage jukeboxes clank into action, couples glide across a dance floor, kids run and squeal and splash, boats thump against their docks. In exploring his past, Timothy resurrects our own and therein lies the tender heart of *Figure's* emotional power.

Timothy and I met nearly thirty years ago. My career as a chef, writer, author, and broadcaster was blossoming, as was Timothy's songwriting, poetry, and nonfiction. We've kept my taxes on track, hosted poetry nights, launched the Gram Parsons Memorial Concert, and collaborated in myriad other ways. We've shared tea and red wine. During a few winters, Timothy loaded up his beloved Ol' Jaxon with firewood for me.

That firewood saved my life. Early one morning, an insistent knocking intruded upon my unnatural sleep. As I stumbled to the door, I wondered how fog had crept inside. I could barely see through it.

"Oh my god, Timothy! My house is on fire," I cried as I opened the door, suddenly fully present and aware that it was smoke, not fog, that filled my house. Timothy ran towards the thick of it, found a wall in my laundry room that was about to go up in flames, and put out the fire.

Had it not been for that wood, had Timothy not forgotten his tarp, had he not remembered that it was here, had he not decided that morning to make a trip to the dump, I would likely have succumbed to the smoke inhalation already infecting me when that miraculous knock snatched me from death's jaws. And now, here we are, entangled again through words and fire, anxiously scanning our big bowl of sky for plumes of smoke, shuddering when the wind picks up, facing an uncertain future, in this precious land we both cherish.

Sonoma County, California
August 2021

**Santa Rosa's Round Barn, built on the Fountaingrove Ranch in 1899, and one of Santa Rosa's most iconic buildings for decades, until the Tubbs Fire of 2017. Photo by permission of Will Chubb Photography.**

# About the Author and Publisher

Because he had no pen, Timothy Williams' love for poetry first made its way into his memory during a long walk on Bottle Rock Road, past the empty hardware store, now a wellness retreat center called Mandala Springs, whose handwritten sign declared: "Honk Horn. Will Travel." Cobb Mountain, California, in the spring of 1970, was his inspiration. It offered time to enjoy long walks and space to appreciate them.

From that first poem, he has written: *Baseball In and Out of Time*; *Gates of Wilbur,* about Wilbur Hot Springs; *The Treasure of Lost Time*, a family book about the hometown of his wife, Sarah Baker; and *Sleepless Fires*, a book of poems published by Running Wolf Press; plus his early collections: *Same Day Different Village, Spokes of a Broken Wheel,* and *Caffeine Makes you Greedy.*

Adding originality to his 30-year accounting business, he developed Jaxon's Press that has published writings and poems on cards for Michele Anna Jordan, Sonoma County's own Solid Air, Doug Jayne, Allen Sudduth, poet Kristine Sudduth, and three poetry books by Jonah Raskin: *Letters to a Lover, Auras,* and *Storm City.* Jaxon's Press also published *Passenger Pigeons* by writer and award-winning filmmaker, Ken Rodgers. On July 1, 2020, it published *Given Enough Time,* the book of song poems by folk legend Hugh Shacklett.

Timothy created and formed Poetry Band with artist-guitarist, Kevin Haapala. They recorded one album in 2003, *Lunch at Lola's,* which includes the song, "Cobb Mountain," that he wrote while visiting his father on Cobb in '91, and the tribute poem, "The Comet and Dry Creek Road." They played at Starview Lodge for his father's 80th birthday.

Poetry Band performed shows in Sonoma County in both musical and literary venues. In 2001, they played for the Santa Rosa Book Fair a few short days after 9/11. Less than two months later, they performed at the Gram Parsons Tribute at Santa Rosa's Old Vic, which was created by Timothy and produced with Michele Anna Jordan and Jerry Hertz, and never would have happened without their enthusiastic participation in Sonoma County's thriving musical culture.

He was a member of Sebastopol's Center For the Arts' Literary Arts Council (LAC), where he chaired for a year. Through the Art Center, with the participation of its members, he produced and performed in Dylan Thomas's *Under Milk Wood*, and for six years running, *A Child's Christmas in Wales* with different co-performers, Susan Bono among them.

One morning, Timothy picked up a *San Francisco Chronicle* and was struck by a vision. He brought the newspaper to the LAC meeting that night and read front-page poems by Lawrence Ferlinghetti. Ferlinghetti had been named Poet Laureate of San Francisco—and it was front-page news! As Chair of the Council, Timothy then initiated a process to select Sonoma County's first Poet Laureate. LAC members Pierrette Montroy, Betty and Ken Rodgers, and Bonnie Petty wholeheartedly supported this new idea. Along with Timothy, they formed the heart of the committee that would ultimately name Don Emblen Sonoma County's first Poet Laureate in 1999. Sebastopol Center for the Arts, and its Literary Arts Council, thrives to this day and remains the home of the Poet Laureate selection committee.[xlv]

These days, Timothy writes and publishes material that explores working, living, and breathing in a conflicted, yet cherished universe. He has been in intriguing and continuous dialogue with accomplished artist teacher, composer, and musician Sarah Baker since 2001; and in 2007, they married in a rose garden in Santa Rosa.

## Artist Statement

Conversations abound in the recovery of tortured landscapes and are overheard in public places— passion for perspective in the 21$^{st}$ century. Some ache for the past. Others roll into the future through their ingenuity and the urge to create a new life just like Mother Nature does. She proves to us that renewal is possible by greening up the brick-red hills in the spring. Once gathering momentum, a transformation into mass wildflower bloom is certain. Though brisk winds keep us on edge, we've learned to build some defenses to prevent creation of the ultra fire. But if the planet keeps getting hotter and hotter, nothing will save us from its fury.

—Timothy Williams

**Sarah Baker enjoys the EcoArts Sculpture Walk.**

I listened motionless and still,
And, as I mounted up the hill,
The music in my heart I bore,
Long after it was heard no more."

William Wordsworth

# Endnotes

[i] <u>Nolte</u>, Carl. "Lives lost in North Bay fires should never be forgotten." San Francisco Chronicle, October 28, 2017, <u>www.sfchronicle.com/bayarea/nativeson/article/Lives-lost-in-North-Bay-fires-should-never-be-12313431.php</u>. Accessed August 30, 2020

[ii] Richie Bucher, Firefighter. *Cobb Mountain Area Historical Society*, Facebook Administrator.

[iii] This phrase, Circle-of-Life Loop isn't found on a street map. It is a name I gave to the High Road to Schwartz Road route. (Like to have a nickel for every time I walked it while still a much younger man.)

[iv] The Switzerland of America, a tourism pamphlet published sometime in the 1910s by the Lower Lake Improvement and Promotion Association.

[v] A century before, families took the journey by stagecoach on Old Lawley Toll Road constructed to accommodate them. It, too, became the route down Mount Saint Helena to carry gold, silver, and quicksilver to the Calistoga rails in 1868.

[vi] The summit of Mount Saint Helena, located in Robert Louis Stevenson State Park in Sonoma, Lake, and Napa counties.

[vii] The Four Nicks was a mountain bar notorious for the occasional black eye.

[viii] The resort's lake was dedicated as Lake McCauley, after Jim McCauley, who built the first resort called Camp Calso. Sometime in 1938, the name was changed to Forest Lake Resort, and the lake, too, was referred to as Forest Lake by locals. (It was also spelled Forrest Lake on the county map.) Hoberg, Donna. *Resorts of Lake County*. San Francisco, California. Arcadia Publishing, 2007.

[ix] Hoberg, Donna. *Resorts of Lake County*. San Francisco, California. Arcadia Publishing, 2007.

[x] John Flynn was one of these craftspeople. He spent his young days at Cobb and was at the center of its working history in the late 50s and 60s. He and his brother Kevin Flynn are Cobb encyclopedias of knowledge through experience.

[xi] The dining room was called the Garden Room. Richie Bucher, *Postcard, 8-24-1955*. Forest Lake Resort, Cobb, Lake County California. "A corner of the spacious Garden Room. Don Emerson, Manager." Stamp, 2 Cents.

[xii] During Sarah Huff's time working at the resort, she met and married the handsome and crafty Jim McInnis, a Jack of all trades, who created landscape projects that recreated natural settings. * In Conversation with John Flynn, January 21, 2021. Cobb, California.
   At our High Road cabin, built in 1962, he built a fountain that flowed out of boulders, and a nearby love seat between trees to observe the water running over stones into rock-formed basins and pools. For years, Jim McInnis did many projects for my parents,

Bob and Muriel Williams and other friends. He traveled to Novato and constructed a grotto with overhead vines and accented it with his trademark panels of stones in mortar. Decades later, while I worked at Yeager & Kirk Lumber Company in Santa Rosa, Jim and Sarah arrived to pick up materials for yet another landscape creation. We talked about the good days at Cobb. That was the last time I saw Jim and Sarah.

xiii The Beatles used to say, "the toppermost of the poppermost."

xiv *The Motley Fool.* May 18, 1915.

xv Billy Catalano had joined Stan Kenton's band in May of 1957 and toured throughout the U.S. Harris, Steven (2003). *The Kenton Kronicles* (second printing ed.). Dynaflow Publications.

xvi In Conversation with John Flynn, January 21, 2021. Cobb, California.

xvii The fire engine was a celebrated member of the resort staff. On special occasions, it fired up its motor and the blast of its sirens were heard throughout the resort. In conversation with John Flynn. 2021

xviii The frog is the tender, triangular-shaped pad located on the underside of a horse's hoof.

xix Rain Bird™ was founded in 1933 during California's agricultural boom. The original sprinkler was designated a historic landmark in 1990 by the American Society of Agricultural Engineers.

xx Vincent befriended me and I stayed at the Tameras's home for a week. He was larger than life, always generous and kind to patrons at the resort. His infectious presence cut through problems that arose seemingly out of nowhere.

xxi Its water was branded Forest Lake and Cobb Mountain Water.

xxii Larson, Elizabeth. *Lake County News.* August 9, 2010.

xxiii Brockell, Gillian. *Retropolis.* Washington Post. Washington D.C. October 17, 2019.

xxiv Elijah Cummings was a U.S. Congressman and civil rights leader.

xxv Jaunita Jackson Mitchell was a civil rights lawyer with NAACP.

xxvi Blake, William. *The Marriage of Heaven and Hell.* 1790. Aldous Huxley's novel *Doors of Perception,* 1954.

xxvii Max Crook, the keyboardist, invented his own electric keyboard called a Musitron, based on the French instrument, the clavioline.

xxviii In conversation with lifelong friend Beverly McGillicuddy, 2014. Cobb, California.

xxix Yeats, William, Butler. "The Old Men Admiring Themselves in the Water." In the Seven Woods, 1904.

xxx In Conversation with John Flynn, a Cobb historian, January 21, 2021. Cobb, California. *Wikipedia,* Forest Lake Resort.

xxxi Hoberg, Donna. *Resorts of Lake County.* San Francisco, California. Arcadia Publishing, 2007.

xxxii Spanish word for stars

xxxiii Call, Alex. "Where the Still Waters Run." *Call of the Wild.* CD Baby, 2016. CD.

xxxiv French phrase for "Never forget."

xxxv I attended a real estate sales luncheon on a day of pouring rain in late 50s with my parents, who considered buying a lot. They declined and later built the cabin on High Road. Map from Richie Bucher, Firefighter. *Cobb Area Historical Society*, Administrator, Facebook.

xxxvi Hoberg, Donna. *Resorts of Lake County.* San Francisco, California. Arcadia Publishing, 2007.

xxxvi Sudduth, Kristine. Poem, "Like a Flood." Santa Rosa, California. Jaxon's Press, 2018.

xxxvii La Montagne, Penelope. Literary Laureate of Healdsburg, California, 2003-2005.

xxxviii Beecher, Cynthia, Helen. *Send Me No Ants.* Healdsburg, California. Finishing Line Press, 2014

xxxix Hess, Peter M.J., PhD. *Cobb Mountain Rising Administrator.* Private Group. Facebook. 11/2/19. "The group exists to celebrate the resurrection of the Cobb Mountain and Valley community from the ashes of the devastating 2015 Valley Fire."

xl Neruda, Pablo. Translated by Stephen Tapscott. *100 Love Sonnets.* Austin Texas: University of Texas Press, 2002.

xli Jayne, Doug and Sudduth, Allen. Song, "A Place Called Home." Jaxon's Press, 2019.

xlii Sudduth, Kristine. Poem, "Like a Flood." Santa Rosa, California. Jaxon's Press, 2018

xliii Firewise USA®'s Recognition Program helps reduce the risk of property loss or damage due to wildfire and is promoted by the National Fire Protection Association (NFPA), which is a global nonprofit organization committed to "eliminating death, injury, property and economic loss due to fire, electrical, and related hazards." www.nfpa.org

xliv Mandala Springs Wellness Retreat Center. "Mandala Mission." *Mandala Springs*, 2021, www.mandala.org/mandala-mission. Accessed November 23, 2021.

xlv The Poet Laureate of Sonoma County for 2020-2022 is Phyllis Meshulam. Lake County's 11th Poet Laureate for 2020-2022 is Georgina Marie Guardado.

Made in the USA
Middletown, DE
17 September 2023

38164930R00073